100 Tips For Keyboards

You Should Have Been Told PART 2

Printed in the UK by MPG Books Ltd, Bodmin

Published in the UK by SMT, an imprint of Sanctuary Publishing Limited, Sanctuary House, 45–53 Sinclair Road, London W14 0NS, United Kingdom

www.sanctuarypublishing.com

ISBN: 1-84492-033-X

100 Tips For Keyboards

You Should Have Been Told PART 2

John Dutton

smt

ACKNOWLEDGEMENTS

Special thanks to: Lynne Austin-Dutton, Liz Walsh, Zak Barrett, Andy Staples, Jamie Humphries, Pete Riley, Richard Pardy, Alan Heal and Iain MacGregor at SMT, and Clare Christison for a lifetime of inspiration.

BOOK CONTENTS

CD CONTENTS

Chapter 1
Track 1 – Technique (1:37)
Track 2 – Dexterity (2:27)

Chapter 2
Track 3 – Augmented intervals (0:59)
Track 4 – Augmented and diminished chords (1:40)
Track 5 – Ear training (1:20)
Track 6 – Harmonic and melodic minor scales (2:27)
Track 7 – Pentatonic, whole tone and blues scales (2:00)
Track 8 – Sus4 and major/minor-ninth chords (1:53)

Chapter 4
Track 9 – Introduction to backing track section (0:17)
Track 10 – Introduction to backing track 1 (0:34)
Track 11 – Backing track 1 complete (2:36)
Track 12 – Backing track 1 minus keys (2:36)

Chapter 5
Track 13 – Introduction to backing track 2 (1:38)
Track 14 – Backing track 2 complete (2:11)
Track 15 – Backing track 2 minus keys (2:10)

Chapter 6
Track 16 – Introduction to backing track 3 (0:30)
Track 17 – Backing track 3 complete (3:06)
Track 18 – Backing track 3 minus keys (3:06)

Chapter 7
Track 19 – Introduction to backing track 4 (1:15)
Track 20 – Backing track 4 complete (2:52)
Track 21 – Backing track 4 minus piano and clav (2:52)
Track 22 – Backing track 4 minus strings (2:52)

Chapter 8
Track 23 – Introduction to backing track 5 (0:45)
Track 24 – Backing track 5 complete (3:39)
Track 25 – Backing track 5 minus keys (3:39)

Chapter 9
Track 26 – Introduction to backing tracks 6 & 7 (0:44)
Track 27 – Backing track 6 (1:39)
Track 28 – Backing track 7 (3:52)

CD voice-over performed by Lynne Austin-Dutton.

Backing tracks 1–7 copyright John Dutton, Jamie Humphries and Pete Riley 2004

INTRODUCTION

In the introduction to *100 Tips For Keyboards: Part 1*, I explained that the object of that book was to give you information that you could then use and explore. *Part 2* is designed to do not only that, but also to bring together everything that book covered in a way that makes sense musically. The most important thing I can put across is that you're not merely a keyboard player; you're something much more than that: a musician. What you do in isolation, for instance, when practising on your own, means something only when you put it into context, either when playing with others or performing solo. To do this effectively, you need to have as wide an appreciation of not just playing but also of music in general. In *Part 1* – which, if you haven't already read, I strongly urge you to do so before proceeding – I mentioned how important it is not to close doors to styles and areas of music you might not think would interest you. The more you know, the more you're able to expand and enjoy your playing, allowing you to discover a sound of your own.

Therefore, as well as a lot more in-depth coverage of advanced chords, rhythms and techniques, this book features several examples – along with backing tracks – of various ideas, as well as illustrations so you can incorporate these things into your playing.

Equally importantly, underpinning all of this is the importance of improving your general musicianship. In real-life scenarios, in order to get the most out your instrument and enjoy as many different playing situations as possible, this is every bit as important as having an impressive technique or harmonic knowledge.

To complement this, the technical area of the book (Chapters 13–15), as well as taking a further look at MIDI and recording techniques, shows you how having an overall picture of what you're trying to produce can transform the sound of your music. As before, the purpose is to introduce ideas and combine the use and choice of equipment to suit your needs, as well as to fire up your imagination to try new avenues. Music isn't just a selection of different areas and components; it's a big, all-encompassing entity which should be viewed as one.

John Dutton
2004

1 TECHNIQUE AND MUSICALITY

'Technique is the ability to translate your ideas into sound through your instrument…
a feeling for the keyboard that will allow you to transfer any emotional utterance into it.' – *Bill Evans*

'I cannot conceive of music that expresses absolutely nothing.' – *Béla Bartók*

You might be asking why we're spending more time on technique when it's a subject already covered in *Part 1*. The fact is that improving your technique is a never-ending journey. A lot of the fundamentals – such as posture and basic hand position – might have been covered, but to move on you must use these techniques described in the first book as building blocks with which to develop the skills you need to get more out of music.

In *100 Tips For Keyboards Part 1*, I explained a few things that might have surprised you, such as the fact that there's a lot more to having a good technique than just being able to rattle off a few quick runs. Instead, it's *how* you do something that counts, and in time we're going to find out more about what that really means.

Technique is basically your body's ability to do what your mind tells it. One of the things a good technique gives you is an ability to do this while keeping a *form* – a good physical relationship with your instrument that allows you to play to your maximum ability. This doesn't necessarily mean performing impressive-sounding, very technical bits of music; more importantly, it's about physically being able to put your own musical ideas into your playing.

Technical And Musical Playing

Music isn't just a succession of notes. In songs or tracks you know and love, dynamics and feel make them come alive and mean something. When you're playing yourself, you can often feel the need to make more of these musical highs and lows. To do this effectively, you need to know both how to do it musically (ie what to do and when to do it) and how to make it happen physically. This is a good example of how technique and musicality are linked together – without the technique to help you play what's in your mind, you'll never be able to do it.

So, first of all you need to acquire the technique and ability to start putting these things – dynamics, feel and phrasing – into your playing. The first thing we'll look at is the use of arm weight.

Arm Weight

To start with, make sure your hand is kept in an arched position with the fingers bent, keeping your wrist relaxed – ie free to move up and down.

Now, someone asks you to play a powerful C major chord straight away. What happens? Chances are, your arms lift up, with the wrist held rigid, and you plonk down your hands on the keyboard as hard as you can. While the sound is probably loud, it will also be hard and won't feel good to play. It's hard to imagine being able to put a lot of feel into music while playing like that.

Now try the other extreme. Play that same C major chord, this time as quietly as you can. If you still keep your wrist rigid, the chord *might* sound OK, but if you then try the same action several times you'll probably end up with some of the notes sounding uneven or – worse than that – inconsistent.

What I'm getting at here is the idea that keeping the wrist free to move up and down is the key to moving on with not only your technique but also your playing in general. If you fall into the habit of keeping the wrist rigid, you'll never really develop your abilities to anything like their full extent.

Let's try the loud chord again. This time, we're still going to produce a powerful sound, but in a different way – using the weight of the arm. Instead of just lifting your arms up all as one, first of all find and feel the notes you're going to play while the hand is resting on the keyboard.

Lift your wrist up and forward slightly, exerting a small amount of pressure on your fingers to lift them off the keyboard and raise your arm up. Your wrist will now be the highest point on the arm. With the arm still in the air, bring the hand up so that the wrist falls down to a lower point. Now combine the two feelings of just letting the weight of the arm fall down to its usual position and the wrist pivoting forward to allow the fingers to play the chord.

As the hand makes contact with the keyboard, the wrist should be back to its normal position, parallel to the floor.

Don't exaggerate and let it sink any lower, and make sure your fingers are bent at the ends.

Try this exercise a few times. You'll feel that, if you allow the weight of your arm to descend on the chord, you can produce a more powerful yet still sweet-sounding chord. It can be difficult to achieve accuracy initially, so don't worry about a few wrong notes at the moment. It's the feeling we're after at this stage.

Now the quiet version. Apply the same principle but this time, when you come down to play the chord, you'll become aware that the speed at which you bring the wrist and arm down has an important bearing on how it sounds. Do this very slowly and you'll develop the ability not only to play a very subtle chord or note extremely quietly, but you should also notice that something is different. You can now *feel*, and anticipate, how the chord will sound before it's played; you can mould the sound in your mind.

Now, of course you're not necessarily going to be able to play this way all the time – the occasions when you have the opportunity to place a single note like this are limited – but what these exercises *do* show you is:

1   How your wrist needs to be flexible and relaxed in order to help you get much more expression;

2   How to visualise and anticipate the way in which notes will sound before you play them.

This is a very condensed explanation of the topic of arm weight. Like everything else, you need to spend some time practising before you become comfortable and familiar with it.

The reason why I've covered the subject at this stage of the book is because I want you to integrate the concept of feel, and touch, into everything you play. When you play exercises such as scales and arpeggios, which can sometimes seem repetitive and boring, you want the time spent doing them to be as useful as possible when you come to play tracks or pieces. Therefore, there's no point in doing exercises mindlessly, just hammering up and down the keyboard; you need to *play* them every time you do them. There are a number of ways you can do this – for instance, practise getting louder and then quieter within the ascending and descending parts of the exercise.

Getting To Grips With Arm Weight

The following exercise is useful as a warm-up every time you play. As you can see, it features a major and minor chord followed by an inverted major chord from a different key to step up to the next chord. Use the technique described above to play each chord. As with all exercises, the slower you do them, the more progress you'll make. If it feels awkward for a little while, just stay with it, as your muscles will soon learn and adapt. Pedal between each chord to make the transition as smooth as possible.

Play slowly, using the sustain pedal on each chord

This is also pretty good practice for recognising accidentals. As the exercise is in no set key, there's no point in having a dedicated key signature. Therefore, bear in mind the primary rules about how you read accidentals, as explained here.

Normally, in a piece which has a specified key signature at the start – for instance, G major and its key signature of F♯ – wherever an F♯ occurs within that piece, it won't need a sharp sign before it to remind you. Any F you see – unless it had another accidental sign (♮ or ♭) before it – should automatically be played as F♯, because it's in the key signature.

In an exercise like this, however, where there is no key signature – all accidentals are written in place – any note that has an accidental before it should be played in that altered state (ie with the accidental) if it crops up again within the same bar. If it *is* to be changed, it will have to be indicated by either a natural, sharp or flat sign.

Where there are lots of chord changes in a short space of time, as in this exercise, it can take some remembering before you get comfortable with this. It needs a bit of concentration to get all the notes right, so use the track on the CD (Track 1) to help you.

Play this exercise at a relaxed speed. The CD will give you a guide tempo.

Dexterity

While I might have given the impression that dexterity (ie being able to play quickly and accurately) is secondary in importance to feel, they should be considered as being intrinsically related – just like most things in music. The techniques you need to master in order to improve your touch – such as arm weight and a flexible wrist – are also essential requirements for developing dexterity, but, like all things, we can't begin at the end; we have to build this ability up in stages.

Get your form right – that's one of the things you really have to make sure of, because if you rush and fail to get your basework right, progress will be slow. I've known some promising players who, because they couldn't be bothered to play anything through slowly, were sadly still at the same stage, scrabbling along, a couple of years later. And dexterity is the same: you can't rush it, even though your goal is to improve the clarity and speed of your playing.

As I mentioned in the 'Arm Weight' section, in order to play to your maximum ability, flexibility is necessary, particularly in the wrist. Put your hands on the keyboard,

ready to play a C major scale. Think about the feeling you had when you played the previous chordal exercise – your wrist was flexible and relaxed. Now, you need to keep that feeling in mind, but as you're going to play a straightforward scale, you don't need to use any movement in the wrist; keep it as flexible and relaxed as possible while still holding it parallel to the floor, and make good use of the fingers.

Play (slowly!) a scale that you feel comfortable with, keeping the wrist flexible but the hand as steady as possible, using just the fingers to play the notes. Try to lift them a bit more than usual, and get to the bottom of each note when you play it. Repeat this – again, slowly – a few times and your fingers may feel as though they've had a bit of a workout. The upper forearm may also ache a bit. That's OK, although be careful not to overdo it.

IMPORTANT: You mustn't feel any aching or discomfort underneath the forearm, in the area where you would buckle a watch. If you do, you're overdoing it and you need to stop and have a rest.

Keep doing this exercise slowly – don't be tempted to rush through. My recommendation would be to start your practice session by playing the arm-weight chord exercise for a few minutes and then run through a few scales, as described above. When building up technique like this, the 'little and often' mode of practising really works, so instead of plodding through exercises for half an hour, you'd be better off doing three ten-minute spells during the day instead.

Practising With Different Rhythms

After a couple of weeks engaged in the exercises described above, you should start to feel meaningful benefits. Your fingers should have acquired a bit of extra strength and your general playing should feel a little easier. The next step is to introduce different rhythms into the exercises to even them out.

This is an area of considerable benefit because, as you're aware, certain fingers have less strength than others. It's easy enough to lift your second finger up and down on its own, but try it with the fourth or fifth finger and it can be a lot harder. Practising different rhythms helps to even out slight but noticeable flaws in timing, particularly when using the weaker fingers.

Firstly, using the C major scale as a reference point, try it like this:

Immediately afterwards, try it like this:

It's important that you play the second pattern straight after the first one; don't do just one pattern on its own. Again, play this exercise through a few times, first one pattern and then the other.

Next, using a slightly longer version of the scale, try it in triplets, giving the start of each group of three notes a definite accent. (The number 3 over the first note in each triplet group is a well-used sign indicating a triplet figure.)

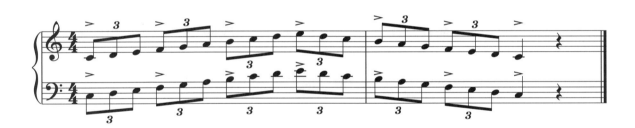

Finish off by playing normally. You'll be surprised at how different this feels after playing in different rhythms.

This technique of practising in rhythms is always useful. Don't restrict it to scales and arpeggios, either; use it whenever you have a difficult passage to play – perhaps a tricky solo. It really does work!

I've used the scale of C major here as an example, but you'd be advised to try the same idea with all the other scales and arpeggios you know at this stage. We're about to learn a few new chords, so incorporate these as well into your practising. I'll suggest particularly useful examples as we go along.

2 MORE HARMONIC KNOWLEDGE

'I had no feeling for harmony... [My teacher] Schoenberg thought that that would make it impossible for me to write music. He said, "You'll come to a wall you won't be able to get through.' So I said, 'I'll beat my head against that wall.' – *John Cage*

Augmented And Diminished Harmonies

In addition to major and minor harmonies, there are other commonly used variations that are essential to know. Many players use augmented and diminished intervals and chords without realising it and yet would struggle to explain them if asked. They're nothing to be scared of, though, and here I'll illustrate exactly what they are and how they can be used.

Notice that I've used the word *harmonies* to describe them. That's because the tones that make up these augmented

and diminished variations are more than just different versions of an interval, scale or chord; they come together to form harmonic colours and a distinctive musical sound.

The Augmented Fourth/Diminished Fifth

Let's recap slightly to help you understand the basic concept of these terms. Back in *Part 1*, we looked at how all chords were basically comprised of a set of intervals. Here's a rundown of most of intervals to be found within an octave:

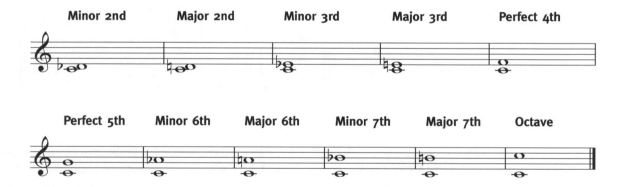

Looking carefully at the above illustration, you might notice that there's one interval not covered. There's a perfect fourth and a perfect fifth, but between those two

intervals lies another note – in this example, the black note between F and G. Welcome to an extremely interesting new harmony...

It initially looks rather confusing, but for simple reasons this new interval can be called either an augmented fourth or a

diminished fifth. A quick rule of thumb: for augmented, think bigger; for diminished, think smaller. That's one reason why

14

what is essentially the same interval can be known by two different names.

But surely this is a bit of a palaver, you may ask. Isn't this a prime example of musical rudiments getting up its own backside? Well, maybe, but the main reason for it is so that it can accommodate the intervals within different key structures. For instance, if you were playing a piece in the key of D major, which has F♯ as part of its key signature, you would write, and classify, that interval as C–F♯ – therefore an augmented fourth. Meanwhile, in the key of D♭ major – which has no sharps in its key signature but five flats, including G♭ – you would regard the interval as C–G♭, a diminished fifth. This distinction might seem like something you really don't need to be bothered with, but as you start to encounter these intervals in different sharp- and flat-based keys, you'll appreciate how the way you think of them affects the way you play.

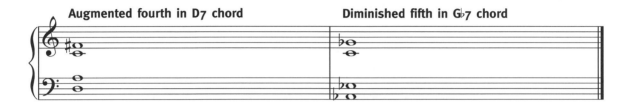

Putting Them Into Practice

Of course, these two intervals sound the same, so despite what I said above, many people refer to this interval only as a *flattened fifth*. At least you know the reasons behind the two variations now. I'll refer to them as aug4 and dim5 from now on. For now, though, let's have a look at the ways in which they're used musically. Play the two notes of the interval one after the other, like this…

…and you can hear it has a very distinctive sound. It was actually at one time (many centuries ago) thought of as something of an evil interval, and was branded by the Church the *Diabolus in musica*, an unholy combination of notes that, it was feared, would summon the horned one himself. It can certainly suggest a dark image, particularly when played lower down in pitch, and it's a beloved tool of umpteen classic rock tracks – for example Jimi Hendrix's 'Purple Haze' starts off with an E and B♭ played together, and you can hear the interval used regularly on many contemporary songs, particularly on the darker, goth-like rock numbers.

A characteristic of the interval is that it sounds like it needs to be resolved. The tension it creates can be eased by moving to a perfect fifth to give this sound:

Resolving an aug4/dim5 interval to a perfect 5th

For an effective example of this, listen to the Led Zeppelin track 'Kashmir' (the original or the Puff Daddy remix) and 'Wake Up' by Rage Against The Machine (the start of the track, which is used during the end titles in *The Matrix*). You can really hear how the very simple change between the opening aug4/dim5 to the subsequent perfect fifth works.

Played As Part Of A Chord

Like most other intervals that have a distinctive sound when played on their own, when used as part of a chord the sound of the aug4/dim5 can be very different. For example, when it's less exposed, the interval can easily lose its 'dark' quality:

Augmented 4th (C-F♯ in the right hand) within a D7 chord

▲ Track 3

You can still hear the interval within this chord, but it's taken on a very different character. This reinforces the meaning behind the second paragraph in this chapter – don't think of these combinations of notes as being merely intervals; think of them as harmonic colours, as much as anything else, that can change depending upon their context.

Augmented And Diminished Chords And Arpeggios

So far, the chords and arpeggios we've encountered have been either major or minor. However, each key also has its own augmented and diminished version. Like the aug4/dim5 interval, these intervals have a distinctive sound and are commonly used in certain musical situations.

Augmented Chord

We'll use C major again as a starting point for an example. A standard C major triad looks like this:

To make a C augmented triad, we simply sharpen the top note (G) by one semitone to G♯:

C augmented triad

▲ Track 4

If you look carefully at this augmented triad, you'll see that it's composed of two major-third intervals: C–E and E–G♯. Wherever you are on the keyboard, if you want to build a root augmented chord, just measure two major thirds above the note you're playing. For instance, in the key of D, a major third above the root is F♯ and a major third above F♯ is A♯. Presto! There's your root-position D augmented triad.

You can form an arpeggio of an augmented triad in exactly the same way as with a major or minor. Using the C augmented triad as described earlier, simply add another major third – a top C – to the top of the octave and play it ascending and descending:

C augmented arpeggio and chord

▲ Track 4

Diminished Chord

Remember what I said about the general rule for augmented and diminished harmonies? For augmented, think bigger; for diminished, think smaller. To form a diminished chord from the standard C major triad, flatten the E and G by one semitone to make E♭ (D♯) and G♭ (F♯) respectively:

C diminished triad

▲ Track 4

Comparing this with the augmented triad – which was comprised of *major* thirds in sequence – you can see that the diminished version is made up from *minor* thirds. You can use this general rule of thumb to find root-position diminished triads anywhere on the keyboard.

However, the way in which a diminished chord or arpeggio is constructed throws up an interesting question.

The augmented chord was completed by just sticking another major third above the augmented triad, which brought us back to the keynote (C in the example). However, as a diminished chord is formed from a series of minor thirds, adding another minor third to the top of the triad brings you to A, while another minor third above that will bring you to the keynote (C again in this example).

C diminished arpeggio and chord

Therefore an augmented chord is made up of four notes, whereas a diminished chord is made up of five.

Inverted Examples

In just the same way as normal major and minor chords have root-position and inverted variations, so do augmented and diminished chords. Likewise, inverted versions are useful for exactly the same reasons: to give a sequence of chords more colour or contrast and to give you more choice when trying to find a part that fits in a group or recording scenario.

Inverted Augmented Chord

If you want to invert either an augmented or diminished chord, follow the same principle as with a major or minor.

Let's take C augmented (in its root position) as our first example. We know it's in root position because C is at the bottom of the chord. To find the first inversion, remove the C to make the next highest note, E, the new bottom note. The C is then placed at the top of the triad to make this:

C augmented triad (first inversion)

The procedure for finding the second inversion is equally simple – the G♯ is put at the bottom of the chord and the C and E at the top. (Note that all these variations of the augmented chord, root position and inversions, are still heard as of a series of major thirds.)

C augmented triad (second inversion)

Inverted Diminished Chord

Using C diminished (in root position) as our reference, and following the same procedure, it's pretty simple to find the first and second inversions. To make a first inversion, put the E flat at the bottom of the chord and the other three notes arranged as follows:

C diminished chord (first inversion)

Similarly, in the second inversion, the G♭ goes to the bottom of the chord and the A, C and E♭ go above. With a diminished chord, it's also possible to have a third inversion, with the A beneath and the C, E♭ and G♭ on top.

C diminished chord (second inversion)

It's very easy to make arpeggios out of all of these inversions, whether augmented or diminished. In addition, take the time to use this bit of knowledge I've given you to discover these new harmonies in different keys; it won't take long and will help greatly in developing your musical ear.

On Track 5 of the CD there's a series of intervals followed by a series of chords. The intervals will be anything from a minor second to an octave, including the aug4/dim5, and the chords are either major, minor, augmented or diminished. Use your keyboard to help you identify which area of the keyboard they come from, and then which type of interval or chord they are. With practice you should be able to recognise them quite easily when you hear them in a piece of music.

Harmonic And Melodic Minor Scales

We've already looked at basic major and minor harmonies, enough to know that the main difference between the two centres on the third note of the scale. The flattened (semitone lower) third of the minor gives it a naturally darker, discernibly different sound from a major scale.

The first version of the minor scale we looked at was the pure minor scale, but there are two more versions of the minor scale that you need to know: the *harmonic* and the *melodic*. Both of these new versions still have a flattened third note, giving them the classic minor characteristic; the main difference between the harmonic and melodic is the fact

that the harmonic scale uses the same notes both ascending and descending (ie going up and down), whereas the melodic follows one pattern going up and another coming down. While you might not see the point of learning another couple of versions of a scale, remember that scales and arpeggios are tools that you'll be using all the time in your playing, so the more progress you make here, the more you'll appreciate that both of these types of minor scale are really useful to know, particularly when you come to play solos and lead lines. They also each have a distinctive sound, which helps to get your ear used to recognising certain types of intervals.

Harmonic Minor Scale

Written out below for comparison is a pure A minor scale and then an A harmonic minor scale.

Pure A minor scale

Track 6

A harmonic minor scale

The two are very similar – the harmonic differs when we come to the seventh note of the scale, which is sharpened a semitone higher than it appears in the pure minor. You can easily recognise the sound of a harmonic minor from the interval between the sixth and seventh notes, which gives it an almost Arabic flavour.

Key Signature

Referring to the relationship between major and minor scales, we know that A minor's relative key is C major and that C major has no sharps or flats. In this harmonic minor, however, we have introduced a G♯, so how can the two share the same key signature? Well, it's taken as a

characteristic of a minor scale that the seventh note is raised (sharpened) so that it's not included in the key signature. Therefore, C major and A minor share the same key signature, and similarly all relative majors and minors share the same key signature.

Melodic Minor Scale

You'll hear many a widdly guitarist practising his melodic minors – as I said, one of the scale's more direct uses is as an element of many solos. It can seem conceptually a little strange at first to have a scale that's different ascending and descending, but that's actually one of the most useful things about it, as we'll see.

A melodic minor scale

Track 6

I've used A minor again as an example here. The first five notes of the melodic scale are identical to those in its harmonic counterpart, but after that things get a bit more interesting. On the way up, the sixth note is sharpened to F♯. A melodic-minor scale keeps the sharpened seventh already present in the harmonic minor, making the last four notes of the ascending scale identical to those in A major. On the way down, both of these notes – the sixth and seventh – are flattened (taken down a semitone) to make a pure A minor scale.

So the melodic minor is something of a hybrid, using elements of the harmonic minor, the pure minor and the major. This is why it's such a well-used musical tool, because it reflects real-world playing. Most parts and pieces of music use a selection of major and minor chords; you rarely find anything that uses only one type all the way through. Therefore – particularly when it comes to soloing – you need to have tools in your box like these scales (and to have a trained ear) in order to recognise and be able to play over different chord changes. Soloing, and improvising in general, is something that can put fear into some players, yet this is often because they've never learned the basics – such as scales like these – that would help them do it. (We'll cover the topic of improvisation in

a later chapter, but putting in the bit of effort required to learn these scales in as many keys as possible before then will help you no end.)

Pentatonic And Whole-Tone Scales

Now we're really moving into the area where we'll be starting to use scales and similar tools within playing. You're not very likely to play music using complete ascending and descending types of scale; instead you'll find that familiarity allows you to take parts of them and then use and adapt them to the musical situation you're in. Most importantly, as you learn these new scales, you're also training your ear to listen and recognise their sound. Later on in the book, I'll be asking you to play pieces with backing tracks that will illustrate how some of these new tools can be used.

Pentatonic Scale

The pentatonic scale is very widespread throughout all kinds of music and is the basis of many tunes from all over the world. Its name gives some idea of its make-up: the word *penta* means 'five' in Greek and, reflecting this, the scale has only five different notes within the octave, as opposed to the seven that appear in regular majors and minors.

C pentatonic scale

Track 7

The pentatonic scale differs from the major scale by leaving out the fourth and seventh notes. The result is a clean-sounding succession of notes that harmonically have a very sweet sound. Like all scales, the pentatonic scale can be particularly widely used as a basis for ideas and soloing, yet understanding it can also be invaluable when it comes

to constructing different versions of chords. For example, try playing all of the notes in the scale above together, as you would a chord. Without the presence of the fourth and seventh, it's quite a pleasant-sounding chord. That's because most of the notes left remaining are part of either the major chord (in this case C) or its relative minor chord (A minor).

Whole-Tone Scale

As its name implies, each step of this scale is a tone apart from its neighbour, therefore allowing only six different notes within the octave. Historically, while also appearing in earlier music, the whole-tone scale became widely used in the late 19th and early 20th centuries within a Gallic-based style of music known as *Impressionism*. One of the fundamental characteristics of this style was the use of music to suggest certain images; pieces often would be given a name which the music would be written to suggest. Composers within the Impressionist movement, such as Debussy and Ravel, made much use of the whole-tone scale. Play it through and you'll hear its mysterious, rather beautiful quality.

C whole-tone scale

Blues Scale

Blues is of course a musical genre in its own right and is the basis for much modern pop music, yet its harmonic characteristics are so commonly found, in all types of music, that it's essential to look at the basic blues scale in this chapter.

C blues scale

The scale is composed of the root (in this case C), flattened third, fourth, augmented fourth, fifth and flattened seventh. Individual notes from the blues scale, such as the flattened third and the flattened seventh, can give any melody within any style of music a bluesy feel. Play a C7 chord in your left hand and, while holding it down, use your right hand to play the blues scale above. You'll hear what I mean about those two notes in particular.

All of the examples in this section are in C for illustrative purposes. Just as before, though, I'd urge you to take the time to explore all the scales in different keys. Get used to the different sounds and colours that this introduces. Tackle them in just a few keys at a time – don't rush into it. You might well find that a scale book – available from most music shops – will come in helpful here; it will give you all of the types of scale we've covered here, with fingering as well. You can combine the use of aids like a scale book to advance your technical knowledge. However, one of the main purposes of this book is to help you then understand how to incorporate these things into your playing.

Sus4 And Ninth Chords

A couple more chord types you'll encounter on a regular basis are suspended fourths (usually abbreviated to *sus4s*) and major and minor ninths.

We'll start with the suspended-fourth triad and chord first. It's very similar to a major triad, but the name of the chord gives you a good clue as to its real identity. Compared to a major – which is composed of the first, third and fifth notes of the major scale – the sus4 uses the first, fourth and fifth:

▲ Track 8

Csus4 triad

As with any other root-position triad, you can add the key note at the top of the octave to get a fuller sound:

▲ Track 8

Csus4 chord

Very often a sus4 chord will resolve to a major or minor immediately afterwards. Try playing a C major or C minor chord after a sus4 chord, as shown below:

▲ Track 8

Csus4 chord resolving to C major   **Csus4 chord resolving to C minor**

The sus4 is often used when a major would sound perhaps a little too bright. It has a solid but thoughtful quality. Like any other chord, a sus4 can also be inverted, or notes can be taken out to make it sound better in a part. (Backing Track 1 [Track 11] features a good example of this.)

Major And Minor Ninths

We've looked at major and minor sevenths already. Once you've understood what they are, it's only a small leap to take ninths on board. To refresh your memory, the 7 in a major- or minor-seventh chord means that the top note of the chord is a seventh above the root-position note. Hence a Cmaj7 looks like this...

▲ Track 8

Cmaj7 chord

...and a Cmin7 looks like this:

▲ Track 8

Cmin7 chord

A ninth uses either a major or minor seventh as its base (depending on which version you need to play) and includes a ninth on top as well. In this chord, however, the ninth is always a major interval (or an octave and a major second, if you prefer) above the root note whether the chord is major or minor. So a Cmaj9 chord is composed of a Cmaj7 chord with a major ninth on top and a Cmin9 chord is made up of a Cmin7 chord but also with a major ninth on top, as shown below. So you can see that, in both instances here, the top note is D:

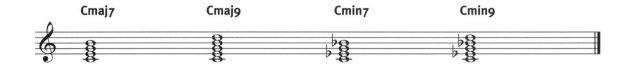

Just to show you another example, take Emaj9 and Emin9. An Emaj7 chord is this:

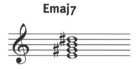

To find the major-ninth chord, simply put a major ninth (an octave and a major second) above E, which in this case is F♯, as shown here:

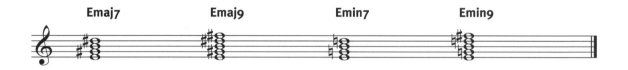

Likewise, to play Emin9, find an Emin7 and, again, put a major ninth (F♯) above E.

3 MORE ABOUT RHYTHM

'I haven't understood a bar of music in my life, but I have felt it.' – *Igor Stravinsky*

'Rhythm is something else than time.' – *Joe Zawinul*

Many of the basics of rhythm – along with the most commonly used time signatures, note values and rests – are covered in *Part 1*. Here, we're going to look at a few more things we need to have under our belts before moving on, and then we'll start to look at how we can use and play different rhythms in various playing situations.

More About Compound Time

The only compound time signature covered in *Part 1* was 6/8, while the other most commonly used variations are 3/8, 9/8 and 12/8. They're all very simple to get your head around because they all follow the same basic premise of compound time: that each bar is made up of quaver-length beats, in groups of three.

So, to recap on 6/8, we know that the first figure, 6, refers to the number of beats in a bar. The second figure, 8, refers to the length of each beat – ie eighth notes, also known as quavers. The characteristic of compound time – that the beats are joined together in groups of three – makes a 6/8 bar look like this:

The procedure for understanding 3/8, 9/8 and 12/8 time signatures is exactly the same. For instance, 3/8 means that there are three eighth-note beats in a bar...

...9/8 means there are nine eighth-note beats in a bar...

...and 12/8 means – you guessed it – 12 eighth-note beats in a bar:

When you hear these rhythms being played, they all have a very distinctive sound because of the way the three beats are grouped together. It's natural to put a slight accent on the first of each group of three, which in turn can lead to regarding each group of three as one beat. Therefore you can often feel that 6/8 has a two-in-the-bar feel, 9/8 a three-in-the-bar feel and 12/8 a four-in-the-bar feel. If you're not sure whether the piece of music you're listening to is in simple time (eg 4/4) or compound time (eg 12/8), just listen for the difference in feel between the two.

Tied Notes In Simple Time

Ties are another important and widely used tool in the realm of rhythm writing. They're not just a technical feature that's relevant only when you're reading music, though; they also help to highlight rhythmically and accent certain parts of the bar.

A tie is shown as a curved line written over two notes to indicate that they should be joined and played as a single note, for the combined length of the two notes. Whether in simple or compound time, the circumstances that make tied notes useful are as follows.

A prime example of tie usage is where a note is to be carried over past the end of a bar and into the next, for example:

The length of the two tied notes is now two beats, but you couldn't write a half note there because there's only one beat left in the bar.

Sometimes it's not possible for a single note value to make up the number of beats required – there's no note value for five eighth notes, for instance, so a half note (made up of four eighth notes) is tied over to an eighth note, like so:

Where a note value is carried across a beat, it's often written down as two shorter note values joined together with a tie. For instance, it's not usual to write a longer note value – such as a half note – on an offbeat. In this particular example, you'd use an eighth note and tie it across, like so:

Notating Rhythms In Compound Time

When reading music in compound time, certain note values are used to emphasise that grouping of three eighth-note beats. We've seen how three beats played in succession are written down, but when writing quarter and eighth notes (and rests) individually there is a certain pattern to observe.

The grouping together of three eighth notes leads naturally to a much-used rhythmic pattern of quarter-note/eighth-note or the reverse, eighth-note/quarter-note, as shown below. (The way that these patterns actually sound gives compound time one of its main characteristics.) Rests are written in a similar manner, with the quarter-note/eighth-note pattern (or reverse) commonly used. Remember that, although compound time is often felt in two, three or four, depending on the time signature (6/8, 9/8 or 12/8), the pulse of three quavers per beat always runs throughout.

Quarter-note/eighth-note rhythm   **Eighth-note/quarter-note rhythm**

4 PLAYING ALONG AND LEARNING (PART I)

Backing Track 1

None of the information in this book would be any use if you were then unable to apply it to something musical. For this reason, while I've already given you lots of information in this book, it's time to bring that into practical use and introduce new subjects by looking at how they fit into typical keyboard parts.

Over the next few chapters we're going to look at five original tracks, each written in a particular style and each illustrating various musical and technical issues. Following these will be two bonus tracks, to be used in conjunction with Chapter 9, focusing on soloing and improvising. Above all, you should have some fun playing along. I've gone into quite a lot of detail with each of them, hopefully explaining some of the techniques that are used in real-life playing.

The main thing I want to explain before we proceed, though, is that you shouldn't try to find a technical reason for everything, because it's not always possible to find one. Most things to do with harmony and rhythm can be explained, to an extent, but when it comes to the way certain things sound and feel, you can't always understand them on a technical basis. Ultimately, music comes from the soul and, like anything artistic, can have a sometimes indefinable quality.

So, while there's quite a lot of information coming up, there are also some things that can't be explained; they have to be heard, accepted and learnt. I'll always try to put a link in to help you understand things in both musical and technical ways, but for this understanding to take place you need to use your ears and explore.

These parts are written around the typical role of a keyboard player in a group comprising guitar, bass and drums. While there may be no tune or vocal part in every track, for reasons of simplicity the different sections within each are known as verse, bridge, chorus and middle-eight. Indications for phrasing and dynamics are given in each track.

As you move through the tracks, you'll notice that there's a general progression in terms of difficulty, but it's not their purpose to take you on step by step; it might be some time before you feel able to move on to the next one. Conversely, don't consider the information given in the earlier, easier examples as being over-simplistic; there's a lot of useful stuff in there, too.

Using Backing Track 1

The main subjects we'll concentrate on in this track are:

- Voicings and use of sus4 chords (root position and inverted);

- Arm weight;

- Use of the sustain pedal.

Sound used: Piano.

Backing Track 1

Tempo ♩ = 93

Verse

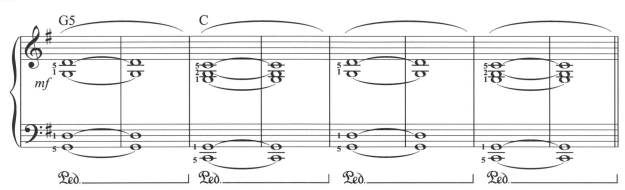

Bridge

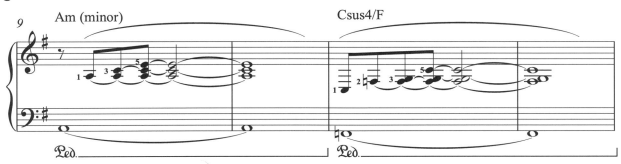

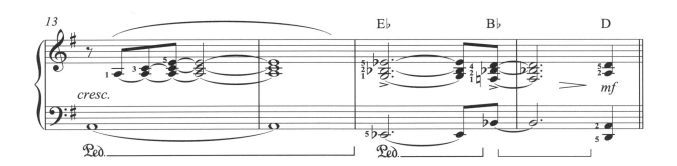

Second verse

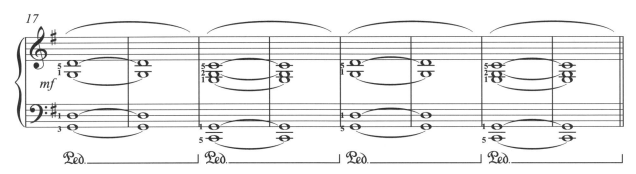

Second bridge

Middle-eight

Third verse

End bridge

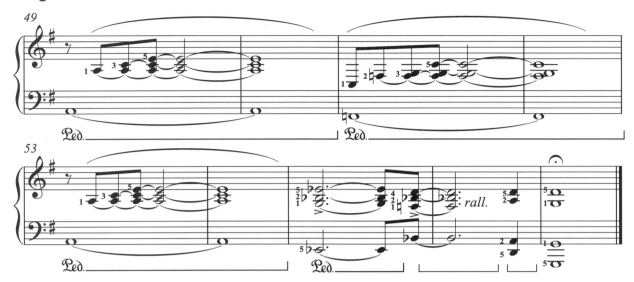

There's quite a lot of information on each topic covered in this piece, so don't try to take it all in at once. Instead, concentrate on each new subject in turn and try to understand what it means before moving on. It might surprise you to realise that all this detail goes into making up a part, but don't be over-awed; just take things gradually and always use your ear to recognise and take in as many things as possible.

First of all, listen to the complete track all the way through. Then look through the keyboard part. The only sound you'll need is a piano, and playing the notes should be pretty straightforward in most respects. In fact, you might think it's a little too sparse, too straightforward. This is where many people – some of them good players, too – come unstuck. Rule number 1 when playing – particularly along with other people – is that you should only do what the track needs. You might be able to rattle off fantastically quick exercises and have a harmonic knowledge that greatly outstrips what you need to use there and then, but unless it's suitable for what you're playing at that time, forget it! You'll just be a liability, and an unmusical one at that.

One of the things it can take longest to learn is what *not* to play, and that's not as easy as it sounds. Sometimes the hardest thing to do is find a really simple but effective part that sounds right. Don't feel you have to over-play to sound good. In fact, the reverse is true. Of course it's useful to have as wide a range of ability as possible, but don't underestimate the importance of economic playing, especially when combined with a good touch and feel.

While this part might be straightforward to play, I want you to understand as much about it as possible. To this

end, I've put chord symbols over each new chord to provide a quick means of reference. It's quite common for a keyboardist to have to play from a chord chart that doesn't involve manuscript at all, so you can view the previous pages of manuscript as my interpretation of how I would play those chords. I'll explain why they suit the part in a little while.

IMPORTANT: Where there's a lot of repetition in the part, chord symbols are not repeated over chords that recur several times.

Overview

Before anything else, I want to have a quick look at the phrasing and dynamics of the piece. You'll see that most of the part is phrased in two-bar lengths. This doesn't mean you have to make an audible break between phrases, though; view them as tiny pauses for breath, something more felt than heard. Dynamically, the part starts off fairly strongly with an *mf* (*mezzo forte*) marking – meaning you should play moderately loudly – and features a crescendo in the second half of the bridge. This reaches a high point at the end of the bridge on the Eb and Bb chords, both of which feature an accent sign (>) to indicate that they should both be marked out.

While dynamic markings should be adhered to, they can be quite general guidelines. It's up to you to look for, and feel, the areas that benefit from more subtle changes.

Voicing And Use Of The Suspended Fourth

One of the things you'll learn while looking at this and the subsequent tracks is how straight major and minor chords sometimes don't give the kind of sound you need. There are many ways to add different harmonic colours, including using new chords such as the suspended fourth. Sometimes

you can also take out notes from a major or minor chord to make the harmony more suitable.

Take the opening chord:

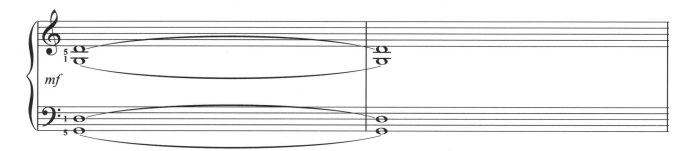

While the chord is unmistakably a G (there's a G as a root note in the lower chord), it's simply two perfect fifths, one in each hand, played an octave apart. A characteristic of perfect fourths and fifths is their clean, spaced sound; the fifths are used here in both hands because they can give a tougher sound than a major or minor chord. With the third missing, it gives less of an overly 'happy' sound than a major yet doesn't give the darker mood normally associated with a minor chord. Try playing a fifth chord next to a major and then a minor chord to hear the difference.

This chord is known as a G5, as it's made up from the root and fifth notes only. Fifth chords are also known to

many guitarists as *power chords* because of their uncluttered sound. With no thirds or other close intervals, these chords are ideal to use with an overdriven or distorted sound.

This complements one of the basic doctrines of keyboard voicing: the lower you go down the keyboard, the less you find yourself using closely spaced intervals and the more you use fifths and octaves. You simply can't hear closely spaced harmonies very well lower down the keyboard. Unless you want to produce a specific effect, using fifths and octaves gives a more powerful, tighter sound – just like it would on an overdriven guitar.

The second chord is also quite interesting:

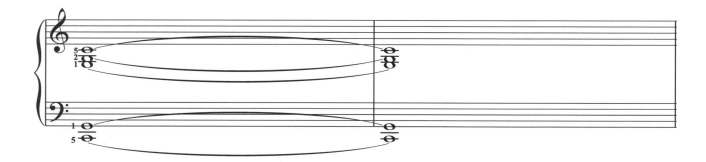

The left hand is doing more or less what you'd expect, but it's worth taking a closer look at the right hand's chord. It's a C chord, following the pattern of the music, but not a root-position chord. As you can see, the right-hand chord is a C major second inversion. Why choose that as opposed to a root-position C?

The best answer I can give is this: Try playing a root-position C chord in its place. It doesn't sound bad – in fact, some of you might even prefer it – but I've put an inversion there because it sounds better to my ear. This is because the colour and mood of that first chord has to be followed by something that, while being a C chord, still maintains that feeling. If I'd used a root-position C,

the jump from that first chord (which is basically a root-position G with the third removed) up to a root-position C wouldn't keep the mood created by that first chord. Instead, the use of the second inversion allows things to stay in the same area, pitch-wise, and keep the general feel intact.

The next two chords – which are identical to the first two bars – restate the introduction, and then we move on to the bridge. In most pieces, following a bridge is normally either a chorus, or a repeat of what has come before. In this case, it's the latter, going back to the introduction/verse section.

Let's look at the start of the bridge a bit more closely.

Bridge

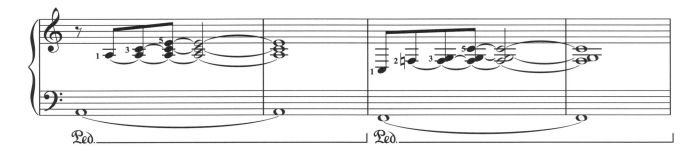

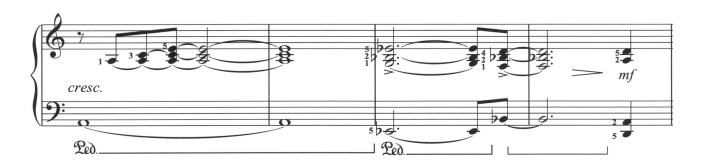

There are obviously changes of chord here, and the track picks up a bit rhythmically. This is reflected in the keyboard part, which has an arpeggiated feel to it, helping it to move along in the context of the feel of the track. The first chord, an A minor, is a textbook root-position version, played as a broken chord (ie like an arpeggio) with the pedal holding the notes on.

The next chord, Csus4 first inversion – or, in other words, Csus4 over F – brings us to the use of an inverted suspended fourth. In Chapter 2, 'More Harmonic Knowledge', I explained that, just like any other chord, the sus4 chord can be inverted or modified, with notes subtracted from it to give a more suitable part when playing in a group.

Look at the right hand in bar 2. It's a textbook Csus4 chord – but, as the chord symbol says, Csus4 first inversion. How do we approach that? Remember what I said about finding inversions in general? A first-inversion chord takes the second note of the root-position chord – in this case, F (the fourth) – and puts it at the bottom. As we're playing with both hands here, we put the F right at the bottom of the chord, played by the left hand, while the right hand plays the rest of the Csus4 chord.

So another (possibly easier) way to describe such a chord is as a Csus4 over F, which asserts that the left hand must play an F while the right hand must play a Csus4 over the top. It's that simple.

Again, I chose to put a Csus4 over F at that part of the

piece because of the sound. The piece is moving towards an F, harmonically, but I didn't think that an F major or minor would sound particularly good there, so I kept the F in the left hand (bass) and looked for a chord to go on top that was close to an F major but without such a bright sound. An Fsus4 wouldn't sound right there (try it – it doesn't!) so I used a Csus4 chord on top of the F bass instead. If you look carefully, you'll note that the Csus4 is closely related to an F major, with only one note being different (instead of an A, there's a G). The end result is that you get a chord that's very similar to an F major but with a sound better suited to the part.

The third chord of the bridge is a repeat of the first, and then we come to what is classed in musician's parlance as a *turnaround*, which is just a name given to a sequence of chords that leads the harmony back to a previous section – in this case, the verse. Here, the three chords that take us back to the verse are E♭, B♭ and D, the last of which is a fifth above the first chord of the verse, G. This movement – from the fifth back to the tonic (the keynote chord) – is probably the most widely used and comfortable-sounding progression to use in such a situation and is known as a *V–I progression* – ie the fifth progresses to the tonic. Look at how many pieces end with it and you'll see what I mean.

Again, the voicings used here reflect the need of the part. The first two chords both feature right-hand inversions, and again look how closely they stay to each other, pitch-wise.

The last chord, the D, mirrors the voicing used on the opening chord of the verse, comprised of two perfect intervals.

Middle-eight

In terms of voicing, the second verse and bridge are repeats of the first verse, so let's look at the next new section, the middle-eight. The term *middle-eight* is used in music to describe a section of a piece that often comes after a second chorus and in many ways is like a bridge, because it has a different musical direction to previous sections. Technically, its name comes from its traditional length of eight bars, but this is no longer necessarily accurate (although this particular middle-eight *is* eight bars long).

When you listen to the complete track, you'll hear that the middle-eight has a different direction. The verse and chorus chug along with a steady feel, but the middle-eight has a burst of brightness absent from the rest of the piece, so the keyboard chords change in character to suit.

The first thing to notice is that they're higher in pitch, giving an immediate feeling of airiness. Secondly, the notes at the top of each chord ascend, giving a similar feeling. So, even though the first chord is actually a second-inversion D minor – which is perhaps not the most obvious choice to put light into a part – this emphasises another, very fundamental point I've already made: it's the context of how a chord is used that determines its sound, not just the fact that it's a major, minor or whatever.

The next two chords are more what you might expect: a full C first inversion, with a C major root-position triad in the right hand, over a first-inversion bass note (remember, it's the very bottom note of a chord that determines its inversion) and an F major root-position chord (although the right hand is playing a second inversion). See how both the top notes of each of the chords and the bass notes in the left hand both move up in sequence? This further helps to give the part a feeling of energy.

Following this, a turnaround takes us back to another verse and bridge, upon which the last sequence of chords end the piece. (Notice the V–I chord progression at the very end.)

Arm Weight

Parts such as the verse section here, which has plenty of simple, slowly moving chords, are ideal examples of how arm weight can be used. What makes a simple part like this make sense musically is the use of dynamics and feel, and, as we've seen, the use of arm weight is an essential technique to help make this happen.

So, going back to the beginning of the track, don't just plonk your hands down on the opening chord without thinking; instead, find the positions of the notes silently with your fingers and then consider how you should play the chord. You've heard the track through in its complete version; from that you can tell that the opening chord should sound solid and make a statement. In terms of dynamic range, we're looking at an indication of *mf* (moderately loud), so at this point you should refer back to the section on 'Arm Weight' in Chapter 1 and practise getting this opening chord to sound strong, sweet and consistent.

While the second chord has to be in the same overall dynamic range, you'll enhance the way it sounds further by making it a little softer, in order to counter slightly the strength of the opening chord. Otherwise, it could easily sound a bit mechanical and, worse than that, uninteresting. Your job is to perform and inspire the listener, so regulate the amount of arm weight and movement you use in order to take the edge off that second chord.

The third chord performs the same purpose as the opener, reinforcing the strong, simple sound of the track. However, while the fourth chord is also a repeat of the first, in terms of notes, think about what comes after it; it leads into the bridge, which is a part that picks up, rhythmically, so the fourth chord needs a bit more attitude so that it doesn't wimp out just before going into the bridge. Use a bit more arm weight and movement to help this happen.

Look at the rest of piece in terms of dynamics and try to apply the new techniques you're learning here to the other sections. The most important thing to do is to think about what you're doing, musically. Which sections are, or should be, louder or quieter? Where do certain chords need to be brought out? Of course, this kind of knowledge takes time and practice to acquire, but the sooner you start becoming aware of these things, the sooner it'll become second nature. As well as listening to the complete version on the CD to help you get things right, become aware of the detail that's in music you listen to every day on the radio, in the car or wherever.

Pedalling And Legato

As you change from one chord to the next, follow the markings and use the sustain pedal to hold on the previous chord for as long as possible, giving you as much time as you need to find the next chord. Remember, once you've played a chord and it's being sustained with the pedal, you're free to move your attention – and your hands – onto the next one, even though the previous chord is still sounding. Thinking ahead like this allows you to consider how the next chord should be played, which fingering you should use and so on.

At the end of the bridge, the D-to-G progression that takes us back into the verse hasn't been marked to be pedalled. There's no real need to use the pedal there; instead, I want you to try to join up those two chords as best you can using normal legato playing. To help you out here, the left-hand fingering is slightly different on the first G chord of the second verse, requiring the use of your thumb and third finger instead of first and fifth.

5 PLAYING ALONG AND LEARNING (PART II)

Backing Track 2

Using Backing Track 2

The most immediate feature of this track, which you might notice straight away, is the compound time signature of 12/8. To date, all of the music examples you've seen have been in 4/4. However, as we'll see, there's a lot more to playing in compound time than just counting the beats differently. A piece can benefit from a different playing style (albeit a subtle one) with a view to achieving a different kind of feel. Now that you should be becoming more aware of dynamics, touch and overall feel, now is a good time to look a bit more closely at compound time.

In addition to looking at this particular use of compound time, the subject areas covered in this track will also include:

* Syncopation and hand independence;

* Voicing;

* Orchestration (using different sounds).

Sounds used: Piano, strings (on second chorus).

Backing Track 2

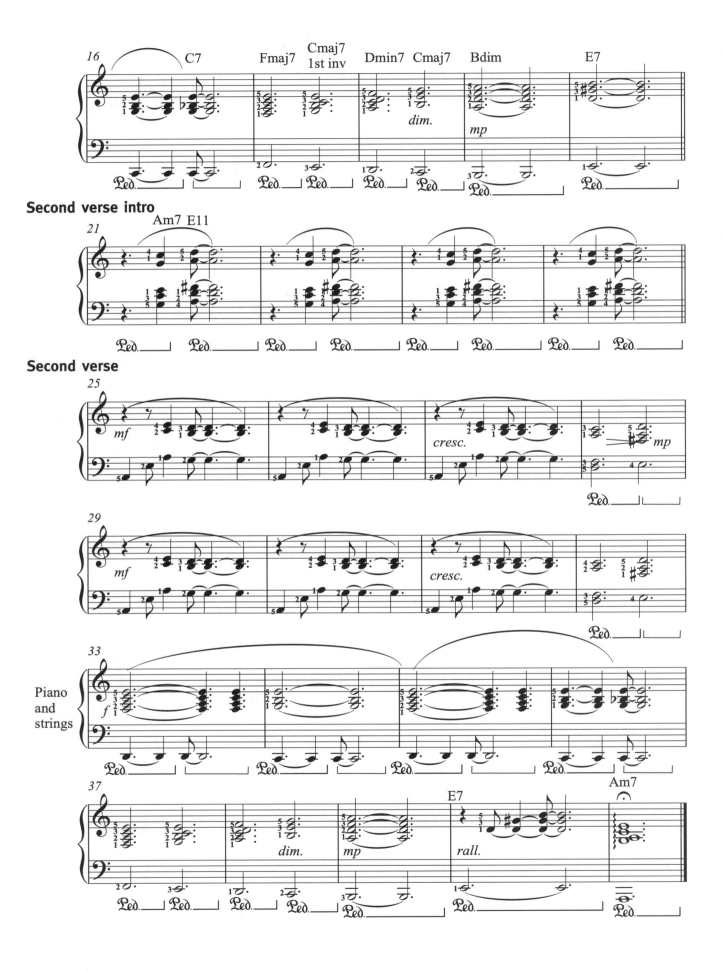

Second verse intro

Second verse

Overview

Dynamically, this piece illustrates a lot of the subtlety possible within compound time. The verses are marked *mp*, or *mezzo piano* (moderately quietly), building up to a chorus marked *f*. The chorus falls away in volume towards the end, on the Bdim and E7 chords. Phrase lengths vary from one to two bars throughout the part, and there is a rallentando (commonly referred to as a *rall*) in the penultimate bar which indicates that the music should slow gradually. A small rall is a feature that's used often when tracks come to an overall stop; listen to the ends of live songs by any big rock band you care to mention and nine times out of ten they will feature slowing sequences of big chords.

This track features a tune, commonly referred to as a *head*. Note the simplicity of the keyboard part; it has to complement the head, not override it.

Again there are sections marked to be pedalled and some not. If at some point you don't need to use the pedal – eg in the verse – it will nevertheless help you to develop your legato-playing technique if you use it anyway. To make the chord changes smooth, remember the basic tips I gave you about legato: consciously hold onto whichever note you're playing until the next one has sounded, without blurring the two together.

You'll notice that there's a new symbol before the last chord. This simply means that you should spread the chord out, bottom to top, instead of playing all the notes together. Listening to the complete backing track will help you understand how to play it.

Playing In Compound Time

OK, you know by now basically what compound time is – a bar made up of eighth-note (quaver) beats arranged in groups of three. As I said in *Part 1* (and if you haven't already read it, I strongly urge you to do so), one of the easiest ways of familiarising yourself with compound time is to hear it, so again you should listen to the complete track all the way through before reading on. It's pretty easy to sense those groups of three quavers running throughout each bar. An excellent example of compound time is The Righteous Brothers' pop classic 'Unchained Melody', which is in 12/8.

As I explained earlier, you can also feel each group of three eighth notes forming a separate beat within each bar. That's why, in a 12/8 track, you can count four in a bar as well as 12. Face it, counting 12 can get a bit tiresome because you've got to count it pretty quickly, so it makes sense to divide it into fewer beats. The feel of the track doesn't change, though – within each beat, the three-quaver pulse still runs strongly throughout.

That division of the bar into four beats helps a lot when you come to play it, too, because it's often easier to feel the pulse of a bar in two, three or four. This translates into naturally putting a slight emphasis on the first of each group of three eighth notes – for example, imagine you had a bar full of eighth notes in 12/8 time. As well as bringing out the underlying pulse of four in a bar, this kind of counting gives each group of three a much more musical lilt than if you just played it dead straight. Try playing that eighth-note rhythm in Backing Track 2 without that slight emphasis on the first beat and you'll see what I mean.

You'll also encounter dotted half notes (ie dotted minims) in this track. These note lengths can be understood just as easily in compound time as in any other. Break them down into eighth-note lengths: a dotted half note is six eighth notes long, so it makes up half a bar in 12/8 time.

Syncopation And Hand Independence

Back in Chapter 3, 'More About Rhythm', we looked at two of the commonly used rhythmic patterns that often crop up in compound time signatures: the quarter note to eighth note and the eighth note to quarter note. The fifth bar of Backing Track 2 is a good example of the first of these. The left hand gets a bit more involved rhythmically in this track, and it starts off the fifth bar with a quarter-note-to-eighth-note rhythm:

Listen to how the first note, A, has that distinct emphasis, whereas the subsequent note, E, doesn't stand out quite so much. Try to feel the quarter-note-plus-eighth-note pulse running throughout each bar.

The next beat follows that same quarter-note-to-eighth-note rhythm, but you'll notice that the eighth note is tied over to the next two beats. The way in which this eighth note feels displaces the normal compound rhythm and puts the emphasis not on the first beat of three, but on the last.

This brings us to a very big topic concerning rhythm – syncopation – illustrated here within a typical playing scenario. Essentially, the term *syncopation* refers to the displacement of the pulse, or beat, within a bar, by emphasising a part of the rhythm that is off the beat. It's something that can be used either very subtly or as a noticeable feature, as in this example.

Here, it can help, when you're trying to get used to playing syncopation, to slow the track right down and go back to counting in 12. Count out loud, and get used to playing the eighth-note chord on beat 6.

Apart from this noticeable diversion, the part otherwise mostly conforms to the standard compound time rhythms described earlier. In the chorus section, however, there are more examples of syncopation. The first one we'll look at is very similar to the first example – in bar 16, a chord is again played on the sixth beat. On this occasion, though, all of the instruments play together on the syncopated beat. This kind of musical device is often known as a *push*.

The second example here illustrates a typical use of syncopation in keyboard playing: using it as a subtle tool to help the rhythm along. Look at bars 13, 14 and 15 – the first three bars of the chorus. This section requires the use of both hands, with the left playing a syncopated note – again, on the sixth beat – against the straighter, sustained right-hand chords.

Again, it can take time to adjust to playing different rhythms in each hand, so try my earlier suggestion of slowing things right down and counting out loud to help you get the rhythm right in your head. Other examples of syncopation can be found in later tracks, but get your head around this one first and get yourself acclimatised to the change in feel that results.

Voicing

Like the one in Backing Track 1, this keyboard part for this track is, for the most part, pretty simple. However, the voicing again adapts to suit the part. In particular, the Amin–Emin7 chords in the verse are comprised of only three notes, as the bass-guitar part is doing quite enough to fill in the bottom end; there's no point in adding any other lower notes to the keyboard part there.

Meanwhile, it's also worth looking at the Dmin7–E11 movement in the fourth and eighth bars. Notice how close the chords stay together, pitch-wise; whereas the Dmin7 is a root-position chord, the right-hand E11 chord is a first inversion. This allows the top notes of the chords to ascend with the bass line – a good musical touch.

A similar thing happens throughout the chorus – the chords don't fly all over the place, jumping up and down with loads of movement in pitch; they stay very closely related to each other, allowing the top notes of each chord to stay very close to, or even exactly the same as, each other. This kind of arrangement can be very useful – for instance, when accompanying a vocal part – so the Cmaj7 chord is played as a second inversion to accommodate this, with the top note remaining an E. Likewise, the C7 in the fourth bar, and the subsequent Fmaj7 and Cmaj7, are all voiced to allow the same thing.

As the chorus draws to an end, it reaches a small high point – a *climax* – so the voicings for the Dmin7, Cmaj7 and Bdim chords are worked out to make the top notes ascend, giving a natural feeling of excitement. (Note the last chord of the chorus, the E7, and that V–I progression cropping up again.)

The short bridge before the next verse is a series of Amin–E11 progressions, using both hands. This shouldn't present too much of a problem, but in order to prevent blurring two chords together, use the sustain pedal carefully. Concentrate on releasing the pedal as the second chord of each bar, the E11, is played.

The second verse and chorus are very similar to the first but feature slightly different voicings to reflect the feel at various points. The dynamic level goes up slightly in the second verse, from *mp* to *mf*, and the second chorus touches on a new subject: orchestration

Orchestration

A rather grand word, you might think, but don't be intimidated by it – all it means, essentially, is the practice of using different sounds and observing how they fit harmonically. As a keyboard player, you have a greater number of potential sounds immediately at your fingertips than virtually any other instrumentalist (although drummers and guitarists also have the ability to trigger MIDI devices these days, too). This means that, in order to make the most of your instrument, you first need to consider how and where you might use all these sounds.

This obviously has a reflection on how you voice a part, as some sounds work better with certain types of part than others. You might also have the ability to play more than one particular sound, or *voice*, at once (if you have more than one instrument, for instance, or if you can split your keyboard into sections). However, because many of you won't have this kind of facility, or will have only one keyboard, I won't go into endless detail here. Nevertheless, it's useful to identify the area of a track where the need for something extra can crop up – such as this second chorus.

In addition to the highs and lows that are happening all the time throughout any track, it often builds in intensity as it moves on through its structure. (You can see this kind of structuring here in Backing Track 2, with the dynamic change occurring in the second verse.) But often new parts and instruments are added in successive verses and choruses, building up a track with different sounds. So it is here – although the piano does a good job on its own for a while, by the second chorus a listener could easily feel the sound to be getting a bit monotonous. Therefore, in order to complement the piano's sound – which is percussive (ie struck) – we can add a different type of sound: a sustained sound.

A piano is defined as a percussion instrument because of the way the notes are played – like I said, they are struck, and after a note is struck, it will die away after a while; it cannot keep sounding indefinitely. A sustained sound has the capacity to keep on sounding while being played, without any noticeable change in dynamic level. (Strings and organs are good examples of commonly used sustaining instruments.) In the second chorus of Backing Track 2, I've added strings in the complete CD version to illustrate the kind of effect that adding a sustaining sound can bring to a piece.

To keep things simple for now, though, you could play these two sounds together, which would mean either having two keyboards (or an extra module) or having the facility to split your keyboard into two sections, allowing you to use one hand to play the piano and the other to play the strings. You can use exactly the same chord voicings for the string part as for the piano, so a straight MIDI connection with another keyboard or module would allow you to layer the sound on top.

Of course, you might not have these kinds of facilities at your disposal, so if you can play only one sound at a time, use a piano until the second chorus and then change to strings and listen to the effect that this produces. Even though this is only a very simple example of orchestration, I want you to start to become aware of using different sounds to enhance your keyboard playing. Although we'll look at the subject in a lot more detail later on, the tracks that follow will introduce further new sounds.

You can start to notice here how voicings, and using different sounds, help you to bring across certain things musically. The purpose of these examples, though, is to get you thinking and learning. There's no substitute for trying things out for yourself, so with voicings, experiment with taking notes out of chords, adding extra ones in and putting together what might seem like unlikely combinations. All the time, your ear will be taking these things in – very gradually, maybe, but over time you'll start to put it all together.

6 PLAYING ALONG AND LEARNING (PART III)
Backing Track 3

Track 16

Using Backing Track 3

We're back to 4/4 with this track, but while the rhythmic base might be familiar, there's a lot of new ground explored here. Firstly, the feel of this track is decidedly funkier than that of the previous two, and secondly there are a few new chords and areas of harmony introduced. The more rhythmically funky issues will be dealt with in a later track; here, we'll concentrate on the more harmonic elements.

Areas To Be Covered

• Use of more advanced inversions and chords

• Orchestration

Sound used: Electric piano (Rhodes). (Also refer to 'Orchestration' below.)

Backing Track 3

Tracks 17 & 18

Tempo ♩ = 88

Intro

Keyboard
(Rhodes or piano)

Verse

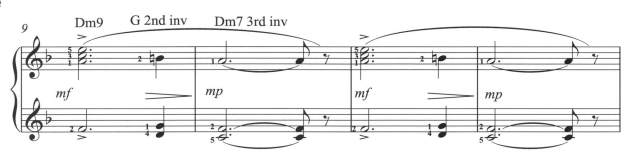

Bridge

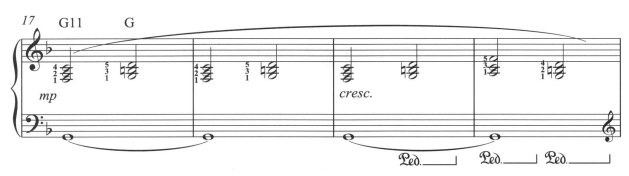

Middle-eight

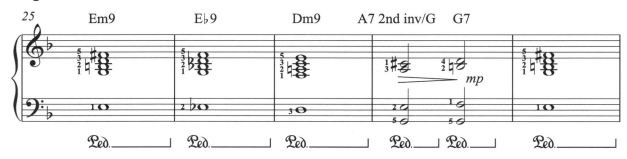

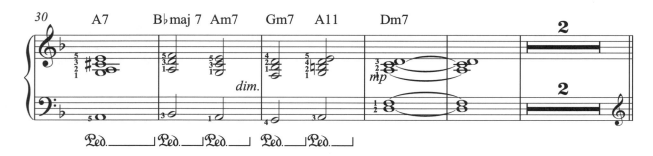

Second verse

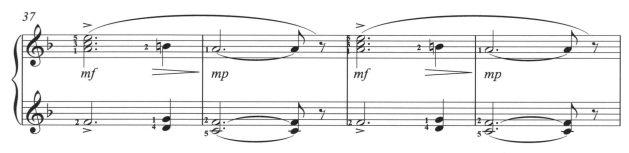

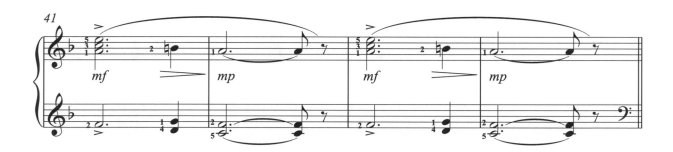

Second bridge

Second middle-eight

Funkier tracks often use more of the jazz-based chords and harmonies. I use the term *jazz* in its widest sense here, because I don't like to bracket the use of certain types of chord or harmony with specific styles of music. Also, you could quite easily write a whole book on the subject of jazz harmony! However, there's a lot of crossover between funk and jazz, particularly when it comes to chord structures and harmony, and here we'll take a brief look at which types are relevant to you and how and why they sound the way they do.

Looking At Funk- And Jazz-Based Chords

You'll find several of the new chords we've looked at in this track – augmented, diminished, major and minor ninths and suspended fourths.

In previous chapters we've seen how the density of a chord – ie how many notes are played – massively affects the way it sounds. At the centre of jazz harmony is usually some sort of dissonance – what might be described as a clash of notes. While these things are subjective, depending upon the opinion of the person listening, intervals such as sevenths and seconds are generally regarded as classic examples of dissonance; they don't make up the normal harmonic content of major or minor chords, and when they're heard on their own, they clash to most people's ears.

As you know, when you fill out a chord – for example, taking a seventh interval and adding a major third and perfect fifth above the bottom note (making a major-seventh chord, as shown in the diagram below) – the dissonance of the major-seventh interval is much less apparent. What's giving the major-seventh chord its sound is the combination of sweet-sounding harmony (the major triad at the bottom) and the dissonant note (the G♯ clashing with the root note, A). Try taking out the G♯ and putting it in again. It's amazing that a single note has that much influence on the sound.

Major-seventh interval on its own and as part of a maj7 chord

As I mentioned earlier, minor and major seconds have dissonant characteristics too and, when used within a chord, can give it a very crunchy sound. Of course, the context of the chord makes a lot of difference to how it sounds, but here's an example of the use of a major second, in an Amaj7 third inversion:

This third inversion of Amaj7 features a minor-second interval between G♯ and A. Again, try taking out the dissonant note, the G♯, to hear the difference it makes.

So, quite often in what sounds a particularly complex or jazzy chord, there is only one note giving it this characteristic, a note that creates a dissonance with another note in the chord. This will become more apparent as we look at this backing track in a bit more detail.

First Verse

The bass and drums play the first eight bars to establish a *groove*, which can most easily be defined as a rhythmic movement that feels good, usually played by the bass and drums. A groove can run through a track (or section of a track) and is often repetitive, giving a 'locked-in' feeling. You'll notice – in the verse, particularly – that the bass plays a lot of the groove around the key of the track (D minor).

Apart from some guitar picking, which is mainly just a rhythmic feature, there isn't much else going on here apart from the keyboard part, so the chords you play need some kind of interesting movement to stop the listener from getting bored. We need some kind of tune, a little theme, that will sit on top of the chord changes.

The way in which the first three chords are voiced allows for this. The first, Dmin9, is played in its root form, making the top note – a ninth above the key chord, D – an E. (Note the dissonant seventh interval in the chord between the root note, F, and that top E.) The two subsequent chords – the G major second inversion and the Dmin7 third inversion – allow the top notes of these three chords to play a theme. I've put an accent on the Dmin9 chords because they need more emphasis than the following two chords, while a small hairpin also indicates a slight diminuendo to *mp* within these two-bar sections.

The use of the G major second inversion not only complements what the bass line is doing, but it also allows us to create a chord movement that contains this little theme on top. This is where starting to be aware of other parts becomes important. Listen to the bass part, initially playing on its own with the drums. (The same bass line carries on underneath the part you're playing.) It doesn't just stay on D, does it? Instead it starts in D minor, moves down in pitch, and then up again to bring it back to D minor. While you could just hold a D minor chord over the whole bar, this wouldn't necessarily sound very inspiring.

Following this opening section, but still within the framework of the first verse, is a small four-bar bridge. Here the chord base moves up to G, but not a G major; instead it's a G11 chord. The sound of the G11 reflects the purpose of the bridge: to provide a change of mood, almost like asking a question. This 'question' is answered by the movement back to the subsequent G major in each bar, and then back to the original D minor groove after the bridge.

The 11th-to-major movement is a commonly used progression – the 11th can often sound as if it needs to be resolved, to either a major or minor.

Middle-eight

Strictly speaking, the middle-eight of this track is somewhat unusual as it occurs twice. It also goes in a different harmonic direction than that taken by the verse and bridge, and it features a tune (or a head, remember). The keyboard part plays a purely accompanying role here, unlike its role during the verse, where it's the instrument playing the most prominent part.

First, let's take a look at the structure of the middle-eight. The first three chords move downwards chromatically (ie in semitone steps – Emin9, Eb9 and Dmin9) and then reach a halfway point. The opening Emin9 is then used again before a sequence of chords leads out of the middle-eight and back into the verse section. We'll have a closer look at all these chords shortly.

The feel of the middle-eight is different, as well – you can hear that the bass part has changed from its verse groove to a more open-sounding, less intense line. With this more simple bass line, composed mainly from intervals of octaves and fifths, the keyboard part has a bit of room in which to use some more advanced chord structures.

Having a head to play against means you've got to think in a certain way regarding which kind of part you're going to use. You've got to move with the head's highs and lows and make the part fit. In this particular section, the head and chords sound distinctly jazzy – straight away, the first note of the head, an A, makes for an interesting match with the Emin9 in the keyboard part. The Emin9 chord, with its top F#, already contains quite a bit of dissonance with the minor-seventh interval between the bottom E and the D

above and with the top F#, a major seventh above the G. The effect of playing this full root version underneath the A of the head results in a very jazzy-sounding chord. With so many dissonant notes, it seems unlikely that it will fit, yet the top A is not as far removed from the Emin9 underneath as you might think. The note A is within the scale of E minor, and while it clashes with certain other notes in the chord, it gives us that effective mixture of sweet and dissonant harmony again.

The head returns to A at the start of the second bar, the chord structure moving to an Eb9 beneath, a good-sounding progression that again clearly demonstrates the way in which the straightforward harmony (the lower four notes of the Eb9 chord) and the notes which give the sound its jazzy characteristic (the F at the top of the chord and the A in the head) work together. There's a feeling of having slightly resolved the harmony with the subsequent Dmin9; it sounds more conventional against the A (still) playing in the head. Be careful that this doesn't lull you into a false sense of security, however, for the next chord takes us into slightly deeper territory:

This is the halfway point of the middle-eight. As we're going back to the opening chord, the Emin9, after this bar, it makes sense musically to use something that will bridge the gap between the chord in bar 3 (the Dmin9) and the Emin9 in bar 5. It feels natural to continue with the downward movement in the first three chords, but we need a sound in bar 4 that will be different enough to emphasise this halfway point and allow us to move back to the Emin9 afterwards. To achieve this, after the Dmin9 in bar 3, the harmony moves towards a G7-type chord.

We could just use a straight G7 here, but I want to introduce another chord as well, to be played before the G7. Why? Well, just take a look at what the head is doing. It goes to a C# on the first beat of bar 4 before resolving to a D. The head emphasises this note quite a bit, and it's possible to enhance the musical effect here by using a chord that will go better with this C#.

Think of the direction in which the harmony is going here. The head is playing a C# while the bass is playing a G. Play those two notes together on your keyboard and you'll hear that they have quite a strong relationship. Amongst other things, they comprise half of an A7 chord. So, in order that the keyboard part doesn't override the head, the chord is voiced with a C♯ as its top note – in effect, it's an A7 second inversion over a G bass note. This then resolves very nicely to a G7 afterwards. Putting an A7 in there complements the movement of the head well, and gives an emphasis that would never have been there had we just used a G7 there.

Bar 5 brings us back to the Emin9 used in the opening bar of the middle-eight, but instead of using the same downward progression as that which occurs in the first half of the middle-eight, the bass line moves up to an A in bar 6 and the keyboard part follows this movement with an A7. This prepares the path for the final two bars of the middle-eight, which take us back to the verse.

Within these two bars is a sequence of four chords that must resolve in order to move the harmony back to D minor for the verse. Using an A7 – such as the one in the sixth bar – would be a possible option as, being a fifth above D minor, it would resolve comfortably. (We've used this V–I progression a few times already in other tracks.)

However, there are two more bars still to go before the end of the middle-eight, and we just can't hang onto the A7 for that long. In any case, the track still feels as if it needs to peak more after that sixth bar. So, as well as moving up to a B♭maj7, the chords change more quickly, each lasting for just two beats instead of the previous four, and the sequence descends to an Amin7 and a Gmin7 before going to an A11 – not an A7 – for the final chord. A straight seventh chord can often fit in similar situations, but in a track like this, which uses some pretty colourful harmony, I think an A11 lends more interest. Let your ear decide whether you agree or not; try putting in a straight A7 and see what you think. There are no hard-and-fast rules governing chord progressions, but it does help to be aware of what different options are available.

Orchestration

Apart from the final eight bars, the remainder of the track uses the same chords and progressions as the first verse, bridge and middle-eight. However, it also features a couple of different sounds running throughout, and these give it a large amount of contrast. While the detailed analysis of what these other parts are doing falls outside the remit of this chapter, we'll have a quick look at what they're doing to enhance certain areas musically.

As I explained during my analysis of Backing Track 2, keyboard sounds can be usually classed in one of two ways: percussive (such as a piano sound) or sustained (such as strings). The keyboard part for this track is designed to be played with a Rhodes electric-piano sound – a percussive sound – but there are two sustained voices that are also used in the backing track.

You can hear the first sound playing the same part as the Rhodes played in the verse part. While it sounds a little like a string patch, it's a much warmer, clearly electronic sound. This, very generally, is known as a *pad* – something that often runs underneath or through a section of music, providing breadth and sustained warmth. It mirrors the Rhodes part exactly – rather like the second chorus in Backing Track 2, which featured strings playing along with the piano.

What the pad gives to the track is depth and warmth. The verse chords are sustained for quite a while in places, and the Rhodes piano would die away quite quickly if used on its own. The pad helps to keep the sound going.

But why not use just the pad? Well, a pad is very good at sustaining and filling out the sound, but it also has what's known as a slow *attack*. This means, very simply, that when you play a note, it's slow to respond. So, changing quickly from one chord to another can lack definition and be mushy.

By using the Rhodes voice as well, however, you have the best of both worlds; while it dies away relatively quickly – as, indeed, does a normal piano sound – it has a very quick attack, like all percussive instruments. While some of the tone of the Rhodes is lost, obscured by the pad, the combination of a quick attack layered with a sustained pad or string sound can sometimes work very effectively.

The second sustained sound is provided by the strings. They crop up initially in the first bridge, where they move using the same chord voicings between G11 and G. Although they might seem to be doing the same job, listen to how the pad and the strings have distinctly different sounds. The strings – more expressive and defined – are used to highlight a certain area (the bridge), whereas the pad has a more general job within the verse, acting as backing to the Rhodes. Once the bridge is over, the strings drop out again, reinstating the original mood presented at the start of the first verse.

At the second verse, the strings play a more prominent part. They also appear in the four-bar bridge section, but here they start to ascend in pitch, moving away from the voicings used by the pad and the Rhodes.

Carrying on beyond the bridge into the second half of the verse, the expressive nature of the strings is allowed full rein in a high *counter-melody* (a separate theme that complements the main melodic movement, played at the same time). A pad wouldn't usually be very effective in a situation like this.

So there you go – a quick look at how a couple of sounds are used here, but one which you'll find useful to remember for later. More than anything else, it's about understanding how the characteristics of different sounds have such a bearing on the kinds of part they often play.

End Groove Section

Because the bass line is such an integral part of this particular track, I thought it would be nice to end with all the instruments grooving around the same line, in unison, so the last four bars don't feature any chords at all. Instead, a left-hand part doubles the bass-guitar line. All the instruments then play together until the end of the track, where they stop in unison. Look at how the syncopation in this bass line plays a big part in helping it groove.

7 PLAYING ALONG AND LEARNING (PART IV)

Backing Track 4

Track 19

Using Backing Track 4

You'll probably get a good idea of where this track's coming from as soon as you hear the complete version of the track on the CD. Recognising how the elements that help a poppy dance track like this work are as important as being able to master the piano part, so while there's a lot of interesting stuff to look at in terms of playing, it's crucial to understand how the various sounds and structures work. For this reason, there are two written parts for this track: the main keyboard part (featuring piano, clavinet and Rhodes) and a secondary string part, which has to be played separately.

The main topics covered will be:

- Syncopation and hand independence;

- Orchestration;

- Playing string parts.

Backing Track 4

Tempo ♩ = 115

Tracks 20, 21 & 22

Chorus (piano)

Second verse (clav)

Third chorus (piano)

Middle-eight (Rhodes)

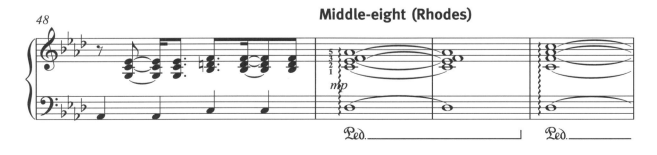

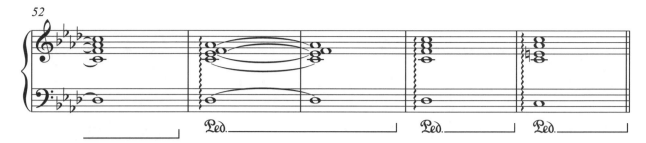

Breakdown

Fourth chorus (piano)

Syncopation And Hand Independence

In order to be able to cover a lot of ground, I've been quite easy on you regarding the separate roles the right and left hand often have to play. A funky dance track such as this, though, gives you an excellent opportunity to get to grips with a few issues.

Intro And Chorus (Piano Part)

The intro has elements of a typical dance-track piano part, and the basis of this section runs throughout the whole chorus. The track is in 4/4, at a commonish tempo of 115bpm. You can hear the bass drum punching away four-in-the-bar quarter notes behind you in the intro. The rhythm of this 'four on the floor' bass-drum part is also taken up by the left-hand piano part – again, a common enough occurrence. This is because an important characteristic of this kind of part is the syncopation taking place between the left and right hands. The right hand may be doing the offbeat rhythmic work, but in order for this to work it has to have something solid on the beat to work against – hence the left hand plays the same quarter-note, on-the-beat rhythm as the bass drum.

While you should be aware what the intro chords are, they're straightforward enough to make another detailed look unnecessary – it's easy enough to see how they're voiced in order to allow the top notes of the chords to play a small ascending theme, while the C11 on the last of the group of four leads into a repeat of the sequence. We're initially more interested with the rhythm here and getting to grips with it.

The most difficult part for many of you will be playing both hands together, mastering the co-ordination needed to play different rhythms in each hand, and fortunately there are several ways of tackling this. The first method I would recommend is to forget about trying to play the part at any particular tempo; instead, get used to the order in which the chords have to be played with either hand. Play the first left-hand note, then the right-hand chord, then the left-hand note, then the right-hand chord, then both hands

together on the Gmin7 chord, and so on. Don't worry about doing it in time; just get them in order for now.

When you've got to the stage where it's a bit more comfortable (and this can take a little while), use the backing track to re-acquaint yourself with the feel and tempo of the track. First of all, practise each hand separately – getting the left hand sorted will be relatively easy and, if you're confident with it, will make bringing in the right hand a lot easier. Co-ordination is your primary goal here, so if the notes are a little scrappy at the moment, don't worry too much about this; just be aware of it for now. The more you practise the part, with and without the backing track, the more you'll find yourself tidying it up. As always, getting your form right by playing things slowly is the only way to learn properly.

Verse Part

This section is something of a departure from previous tracks. The only percussive sound we've used so far has been piano-based, either acoustic or electric (Rhodes), but in this verse part you'll find a part for a clavinet – a very expressive and funky sound. Have a listen to the backing track to hear what it sounds like. Most keyboards – whether electric pianos or synthesisers – have a clav sound, which should bear a reasonable resemblance to the one I've used on the CD.

The abbreviation *clav* can be somewhat confusing, as it is short for 'clavichord' as well as 'clavinet'. The clavichord was a keyboard instrument that pre-dated the piano, used during the Baroque period of music (very roughly 1650–1750). It had a similar sound and action to a harpsichord – ie the strings inside were plucked, as opposed to struck the way they are on a piano. This plucking action gave the clavichord its distinctive sound.

While the piano had become the default keyboard instrument by the end of the 18th century, the essence of the clavichord's sound was incorporated into a (relatively) modern electronic keyboard called the clavinet, which dates from the 1960s. The clavinet is a mechanical instrument, and was very widely used throughout the '60s and '70s, its tight percussive sound lending itself naturally to funky lines and parts. It's also an extremely heavy instrument, so we should be grateful that the sound is reproduced on so many modern keyboards and we don't have to lug around a real-life example!

The verse features a good example of a funky clav part. There are many points of similarity between the intro and chorus piano part here – a large degree of two-handed syncopation, for instance. However the clav has a shorter decay than the piano, and its sound has a more immediate bite, so the part is written to cater for this. In particular, the very short syncopations in the left hand wouldn't really be effective on a piano.

Making It Sound Funky!

Syncopation and dynamics are significant tools within funk playing. However, in many ways their use is similar to that of dissonant and straight harmonies in jazz music – it's a mixture of the onbeat and offbeat (syncopated) rhythms that make the funky lines come alive. So, by analysing the first two bars, you can see that the left hand plays on beat 1 of each bar and the right hand on beat 4. The rhythms in between may look a little complicated, but, like most things, when they're broken down, they're really quite simple.

To get to grips with this part, first use the same method as described for the piano part above – don't worry about tempo initially; instead, get used to the order in which you need to use each hand. It's only a two-bar phrase, so once you have it sorted, you can concentrate on the musical aspects needed to make it sound funky. (Refer to the CD if you need some help here.)

When you've got both hands doing the correct thing in the correct places, break the 4/4 time signature down and count each bar slowly in 16. This is the easiest way to feel comfortable about where the various notes and rests occur in the bar.

When you've mastered this stage, it's time to put some dynamics in. Because the part is in a range that could be written in either treble or bass clef, I've written the first verse in the treble clef and the second verse in the bass clef, giving you a chance to practise reading your leger lines.

Dynamics

As you now know, dynamics help to make a piece of music out of what would otherwise be a series of notes. Sometimes a part will give you a host of directions to follow, while at other times you might need to use your intuition and experience. Here, this clav part requires you to do a little of both.

I've marked some notes with accents, the first being

the opening left-hand F. There is also a slur between the two right-hand 16th notes on the second beat, indicating that there should be an emphasis on the first note(s). (Using slurs like this can be useful where an accent would be too strong a dynamic marking.)

Equally important is knowing how to play the little offbeat notes in between. Consider for a minute their purpose: they help to carry the rhythm along, without necessarily being too prominent. For an accented rhythm to work, whether it's syncopated or not, it needs a contrasting, unaccented part to play against, so these little 16th offbeat notes in beats 1 and 2 should be just a rhythmic presence, playing what is essentially a supporting role – although a very important one, nevertheless. As an experiment, take them out and hear what this section sounds like.

The really accented syncopated bit is the right-hand chord played at the end of beat 2 (or beat 8 if you're counting in 16) – it's tied over to the next beat, meaning that there's nothing playing directly on beat 3. There's an accent here as well to remind you to bring it out. To counter this accent, the chord that follows it should be much less prominent.

Another thing worth noting is the sharp rhythmic nature of the 16th notes in this two-bar phrase. This is where the sound of the clav comes into its own. Just as the chords above need a dynamic opposite in order to be effective, the more sustained chords and notes need rhythmic opposites to achieve the same kind of distinction. So the right-hand chord that follows the syncopation – played on beat $3^1/2$ – benefits being from not only dynamically reduced (quieter) but also shorter.

Another place which features a slur, indicating a slight emphasis, is at beat 4, on the first of the group of four right-hand 16th notes. In fact, try not only to make this first note a little more prominent, but also to play the subsequent three notes each a little softer, so that there's a slight feeling of the phrase dying away towards the end of the bar.

All this might seem to be quite a bit of detail for just two bars of rhythm, but the principle behind most of it is fairly understandable. As I explained, for accents and highlights to work, they need a counter – an opposite – against which to work. With many 16th-note passages, you can hear this happening several times within the space of a bar.

A good way of expanding your understanding of this is to listen to the drummer's hi-hat part within the backing track. Hear how much it rises and falls, noting all the little syncopations and accents that make the part work. It's possible to analyse the rhythm of this piece to a much greater extent than we have space for here, but, as I said, some things you can't precisely explain why they work and sound right. Most importantly, then, listen and be aware of as much as possible.

Technique

It can help to have some pointers to help you play with a clav sound in this kind of style. While the clav and piano are similar, insofar as they are both percussive sounds, the clav responds differently, both in terms of touch and sustain. The extra initial bite that a clav has over a piano leads to a naturally more aggressive playing action, often brought out well with very short rhythms. While it hasn't got the tone and sustain to play the big chords that a piano can, the sharper response the clav possesses – even when playing quieter notes – makes it an extremely intricate sound.

Arm Weight

Even more noticeably than with a piano, the sound of the clav benefits from the use of arm weight and a relaxed wrist. Because of the kind of action you need to accent chords and notes, you can't afford to hold your wrist rigid; the extreme dynamic range of the clav demands that, when going from sharp accents to very short, quieter single notes, you might need to shape the sound more than usual, using the movement of the hand and wrist. I've seen plenty of clav players attack the keyboard furiously, wasting energy and creating tension in their playing. Try not to do this. Instead, remember that keeping your form intact and staying relaxed will mean that you can make progress and improve this area of your playing and others. In addition, this technique will allow you to be far more effective, dynamically, which means your playing will sound more exciting and musical. You can therefore allow yourself a bit more movement when playing accented notes and chords.

Take the first note – the F in the left hand – for example. Keep in mind the technical basis of using the correct arm weight, but use less of the arm and accelerate the speed at which the wrist pivots down to strike the key. Too much arm weight will lead to an unnecessary amount of movement and make things a bit unwieldy. With practice, you can get a snappy yet solid-sounding touch that still allows you complete control over the sound.

At the other end of the spectrum, it can be beneficial to reduce the amount of finger movement when playing a quieter note, such as one of the unaccented offbeat 16th notes in bar 17 (fourth or fifth notes). One of the features of the clav is that, even when playing low in the dynamic range, the percussiveness of the note still comes across. Therefore, in order to take advantage of the clav's sensitivity, it can help to use just very small finger movements so that these notes don't come out too loudly. Make sure that you reach the bottom of the key's travel, though; don't skate on top of it, or it'll be harder to get a consistently accurate sound.

Orchestration

There's quite a lot going on in this track, with the piano, clav, Rhodes electric piano (in the middle-eight) and strings all playing a role. The piano and clav's roles have been discussed already, while the Rhodes acts as a nice release in the middle-eight, but it's the string part I really want to have a look at here and analyse in a bit more detail.

Playing String Parts

First, it's important to understand a few things about strings. The stringed instruments that the string sounds on your keyboard or synth try to emulate come in various sizes and, correspondingly, play in different pitch registers.

The four principal stringed instruments used in a modern orchestra are double basses (low register), cellos (lowish to middle registers), violas (middle to highish registers) and violins (highish to high registers). The registers in which these various instruments play are determined by each instrument's size and the lengths, thicknesses and tension of its strings. The lowest-register stringed instrument – the double bass – is the largest, with the thickest strings and the least tension, while the highest-sounding – the violin – is the smallest, with the thinnest strings and the most tension. These are important factors to take into account because, when you use a string sound at a certain pitch, it helps to have an idea of what the real instrument does in order for your keyboard playing to be as convincing as possible.

Your keyboard may have a selection of string sounds, from solo instruments to whole string sections. Put bluntly, the replication of solo stringed instruments doesn't generally work that well – not necessarily because the sound is poor (although it often can be), but rather because the way in which a real stringed instrument is played is totally different to the way in which a keyboard is played. A string player uses a bow to make contact with his instrument, drawing it across the four strings. He can therefore do something that a keyboard player can't easily do: change the dynamics of a note while playing it.

Because of this (and a few other factors), you need to use string sounds carefully if they are to sound good. Generally speaking, use section sounds as opposed to solo instruments, and accept that while some parts sound great with real strings, they won't necessarily work very well when played with the string patch on your keyboard.

The next stage is to look at some of the key elements of string playing and how to adapt them into the keyboard part described in Backing Track 4.

INTRO AND CHORUS

In real life, this kind of part would be played either by violins or, possibly, violins and violas. Its role is to provide a theme, featuring a mixture of sustained and energetic, arpeggiated notes.

There are a few ground rules which you should try to stick to when using string sounds generated by a keyboard. Firstly, bowed string patches tend to be one of two distinct types: either *agitato* (quick attack), which is best for playing the energetic stuff, or *legato* (slower attack), a smoother, lusher sound better suited for themes, tunes or sustained pads. Agitato patches on keyboards can work well in certain situations, but, because of they way in which they make that initial bite of the note as responsive as possible, their usefulness really extends only to sections where you need a heavily marked, accented part. While the legato sound is far more generally useable, its downside is that its inherently slower attack can make quicker passages sound untidy and laboured.

Ideally, you'd have a cross between the two, and while it's possible to construct patches that use both types of sound, the real problem lies in using the keyboard as a control surface; having to strike a key means that you can't always combine some sounds together effectively. In a recording environment, where you can layer up and mix together a variety of agitato and legato sounds, this can be less of a problem, whereas playing live is more tricky.

Because the string part on this backing track contains a large number of sustained notes, it's no use trying to get away with an agitato sound, even though the quicker passages would benefit from a snappier response. Therefore, use your most responsive legato sound in order to minimise the effect of the slow attack.

Playing the part in octaves can often help to add substance to higher notes. The higher you play string sounds on your keyboard as single notes, the weedier they can sound, while adding the same part an octave down can make it a lot more substantial. Sometimes, trying the two sounds a couple of octaves apart can work well, particularly when playing a lot of sustained notes. In this track, both hands play exactly the same notes, although they're an octave apart.

BOWING

The opening four bars feature a mixture of long sustained notes and quick descending lines. The legato sound deals well with the longer notes, but the quicker ones need a bit of attention to prevent them from lagging behind. The problem can be minimised by using phrasing and dynamics to make the line more string-like.

Certain highs and lows happen naturally when playing

a stringed instrument. Many of these are influenced by the way in which the bowing is arranged. Without going into excessive detail (although a small amount of extra knowledge is helpful here), as the bow is drawn back and forth across the string, the stroke where the bow hand starts nearest the instrument is known as a *downbow*, whereas the opposite stroke is known as an *upbow*. At the start of a bar, or on an accented chord, it's generally most common to use a downbow, as it's the more forceful and dominant stroke. While an upbow can also be used in these kinds of circumstances, in order to help you to envisage the kind of playing action and phrasing that results, we'll keep things very simplistic and regard the upbow as a precursor to the downbow, used to lead up to a musically more climactic event.

Bowing also has a major effect on the type of sounds produced, whether legato or agitato. Smooth bowing – sometimes playing several notes within a single stroke (up or down) – obviously lends itself to legato playing, while single, vigorous strokes – usually using a separate up- or downbow for each note – produce a much more urgent sound.

A real string player uses a combination of smooth legato playing and shorter, more agitato strokes. It's necessary here to find the areas where a string player would join up certain notes in a legato way, and other areas where he would be more likely to use single, shorter bows to give a more urgent sound. Believe it or not, one of the more useful things to do here is to hum the part; if you do this, it's actually quite difficult to avoid putting in phrasing points and feeling where natural and dynamic ups and downs occur.

PRACTICAL STRING PLAYING

Look at the chorus string part on the next page. To make this part sound as convincing as possible, from a keyboard player's perspective, you need to look for groups of notes – two, three, four or five at a time – that can be joined up and slurred (ie playing legato) and the notes that need a shorter, more staccato touch.

After the long, sustained first note, it feels natural to phrase the next one – the E♭ – staccato, but the two after that are good examples of where to join up and play legato. As the first of these notes, F, is the more dominant of the two, give it a slight accent (indicated by the slur), with the second note tailing away – imagine the end of a downbow stroke, with the natural emphasis on the earlier, stronger part of the stroke. To counter this, the following E♭ needs to be phrased separately (play it as short as you can) before the subsequent two notes – the B♭ to C – are phrased together.

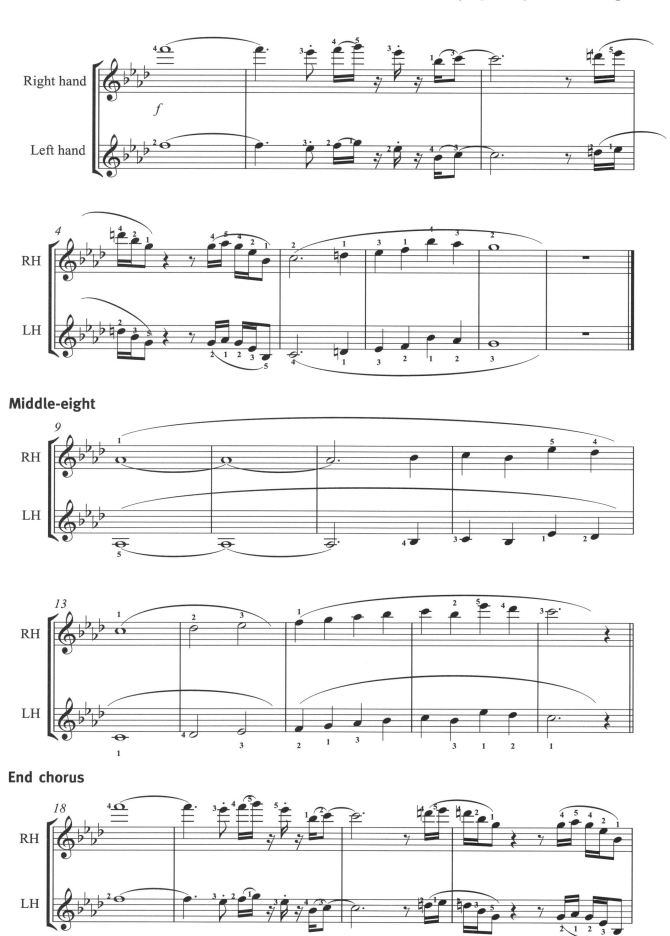

Middle-eight

End chorus

This precedes the descending 16th-note line at bar 4. Think about how you'd hum that – you wouldn't emphasise every single note, would you? It feels more natural to phrase them all together, to think of them as being joined up in a single bow. With this in mind, play these five notes legato, as a single line.

A similar rhythmic pattern crops up in the next bar, where a similar series of five 16th notes is phrased together, the notes naturally falling into a legato style. The part then uses a series of sustained notes to create a little theme, bringing the chorus to an end. Hum it and you'll hear the legato phrase that joins up these long notes.

The string part then takes over and becomes the main point of interest in the middle-eight, playing a theme of smooth, sustained notes. Obviously, this needs a legato approach – look at the lengths of the phrases, which are split up into two-, three- and four-bar sections. The end chorus is very similar to the first and second choruses, with a few minor changes in notation.

General Approach

Paying this kind of attention to phrasing is one of the most helpful things you can do when trying to make a string part sound convincing. Generally, a legato string sound is going to drag slightly, due to its slow attack, so you'll need to approach quicker passages in a certain way, pinpointing the notes to group and play together in a legato way and the staccato-type notes to counter them. Highlighting these legato and staccato notes is a big step towards making the sound as realistic as possible.

8 PLAYING ALONG AND LEARNING (PART V)

Backing Track 5

Track 23

Using Backing Track 5

This next track might seem like the most advanced so far, and in some ways it is, exploring further aspects of rhythm and harmony. Instead of thinking of it in those terms, though, you should view it as just another batch of information that you can use in your own playing – nothing more.

Backing Track 5 uses only a piano sound, allowing you to concentrate more on the playing side of things rather than on production and using other sounds. In terms of style, it's based around a retro '70s-type groove, with a distinctive swung-triplet rhythm running throughout.

Two elements make this particular type of triplet feel stand apart from previous examples in compound time: the swung feel coming from the repetitive eighth-to-quarter-note figure (such as the opening left-hand figure) and the snare-drum beat occurring on beat 3 rather than on beats 2 and 4. When the main beat falls on 3 like this, it's usually referred to as having a *half-time feel*.

To reflect all of these rhythmic characteristics, the time signature is based in 4/4 rather than 12/8.

The accent on the third beat creates a very different feel in itself compared to the previous examples, giving the impression of the track being at a slower tempo and having quite a bit of space.

The key signature, E♭ minor, has quite a large number of accidentals. Remember that you've got six flats when you start to read the chords or some of them might sound a little odd...

Backing Track 5

Tempo ♩ = 120

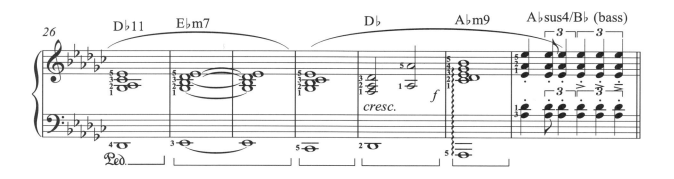

Second verse

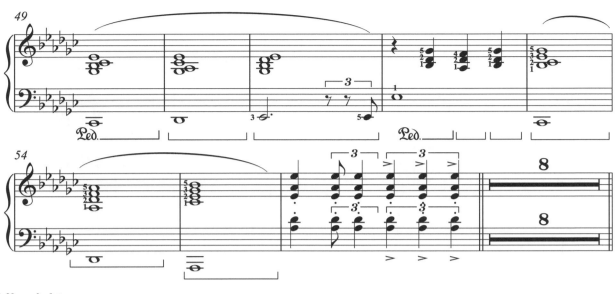

Middle-eight

Third verse

Third chorus

Main Keyboard Groove (Verse)

Because this four-bar sequence is used as a basis for much of the whole track, it's worth separating the track into three sections – this part, the bridge and the middle-eight – and looking at the interesting points of each in more detail. I've written in two possible voicings here, both of which are very similar to each other, apart from one note. The preferred version is this one...

...which you might find a bit of a stretch. While I want you to try to play this version, you might have to work up to it, so as a substitute you can make things a bit easier by playing an E♭ with the thumb rather than the D♭, as shown here:

If you find this difficult to play, too, try breaking it down while practising and just play it in its broken form, as an E♭ minor arpeggio. After a while your fingers will adjust to the spacings between the notes and you'll find it much easier to manage playing it as a chord. Likewise, this is

the best way to work up to the larger version of the chord: play it as an arpeggiated series of notes until your stretch improves. Of course, if you make sure you practise your arpeggios on a regular basis, this will be much more manageable for you anyway...

In Chapter 11, 'Tips And Workouts', there are a few suggestions listed that will help you to improve the size of your stretch.

Syncopation And Two-Handed Rhythm Playing

The rhythmic element is one of the most important elements of this part. Syncopation occurs again here in bar 1 with the main emphasis being off the third beat, but more notably it's the interaction between both hands that makes the part really work. With a triplet rhythm, as we've seen in the earlier 12/8 track, it feels natural to accent the first of a group of three eighth notes. This natural emphasis carries through to the swung eighth-note-to-quarter-note rhythm in this track. When coupled together, because the rhythmic pulse is centred around the eighth note, the quarter note must play a supporting role without detracting from the accent on the eighth note. (As well as listening to the keyboard part on the complete version on the CD, try to pick out the drummer's hi-hat part to hear a good example of this kind of playing in action.)

You'll find that keeping a good flow of this eighth-note-to-quarter-note rhythm can be difficult to achieve when one hand is playing a heavily chordal part. To make the whole process smoother and more varied, you need to use both hands. Let's look at how this happens in the main verse groove:

Within this main groove we have examples of both syncopation and the sharing out of rhythmic duties between the right and left hands. The syncopation is easy to spot: the big right-hand chord just anticipating the third beat of the first bar. After this syncopated chord, the left

hand anticipates the next right-hand chord, playing a subtle but very effective triplet eighth note before it. The left hand then picks up the rhythm and keeps the flow of the track going. This figure is then reprised in the fourth bar, where it serves the same rhythmic purpose, although here the left hand plays a different note to accommodate the change in chord.

This is a simple example of using both hands to generate syncopated interest, but it's a common technique used within all time signatures and genres.

Other syncopation worth pointing out is in the middle-eight section, where eighth notes anticipate the start of the second, fourth and sixth bars. You can see there how using tied notes (ie those that are held over) helps to make these syncopations work.

Dynamics

The dynamic approach to the verse part is determined by two main features: the natural accents that occur within the triplet feel and the division of the eight bars into four separate phrases.

There are two points within the first bar of the verse that act as a focus: the first beat – brought in with the left-hand eighth-note-to-quarter-note rhythm – and the syncopated chord just in front of the third beat, which is (dynamically speaking) the high point of the bar. Therefore, both of these points need to be marked out. On that first beat, there's a slur over the first two notes which puts the emphasis on the first, lower E♭, with the E♭ an octave above it not as prominent. This keeps the natural feel of the quarter-note-to-eighth-note rhythm flowing.

Correspondingly, the syncopated right-hand chord must also reach a dynamic high point. In order to bring this about, the previous right-hand chord is played slightly more quietly in order to allow the second chord to make more of an impact. (Note as well the staccato marking on the second chord.)

The second bar is the answer to the first bar's question. Apart from the subtle left-hand eighth note, it's more rhythmically straightforward, so its musical interest stems from the dynamic level at which each chord is played, which in turn is related more to the length of the phrase than anything else. The end of a phrase is similar to the end of a breath: having made a point, it falls away slightly at the end. So, while the three chords ascend in pitch, they reach a dynamically high point on the main, third beat, and the final chord then drops in volume, tailing off slightly.

This question-and-answer feeling is carried over to the third and fourth bars, with the third bar a repeat of the first. However, the fourth bar – while similar to the second – differs slightly in that there is no separate chord on the fourth beat; instead, the B♭min7 chord played on beat 3 is held over until the end of the bar. Nevertheless, this third-beat chord also needs to end the phrase, so it must be held back slightly, in terms of volume.

Technique

In order to put these points into practice successfully, it's essential to keep developing your playing with regard to arm weight and wrist flexibility. Otherwise, you simply won't manage it as well as you might.

Here's a quick tip to help you play the opening left-hand sequence. The two E♭ notes an octave apart don't pose a particular problem in themselves, but remember that each of these two notes must have a distinctive feel, with the emphasis on the first note. The second note then needs to tail off slightly. With this in mind, it will help here to touch on something called *rotation*, which is basically a very simple technique allowing the hand to rotate slightly from left to right – in this instance, helping you to play the second note more quietly and accurately by making the speed of rotation slower. This won't work if you're holding tension in your wrist, so be aware of this and adjust your hand accordingly. Whenever you have to play a sequence of notes that involves a fairly large stretch, like this passage, this technique can be used to help with both accuracy and tone.

Try to make sure you play the large right-hand chord in the verse with your wrist as relaxed as possible. Because of the stretch involved, this might be difficult for a while, but, as with all things, keep going and you should soon notice the progress you're making.

Be aware that the next chord should be played with a staccato touch. To help maintain the tone of the chord while doing this, use more of your wrist rather than moving your arm and bring the wrist up slightly as you play it. The resemblance between the second and fourth bars makes for a similar approach, technically: a relaxed wrist, not too much arm movement and a slight upward lift of the wrist to tail off the last chord.

Voicing

That opening right-hand chord in the verse is quite interesting – basically, it's an upside down E♭min7. You could use quite a straightforward substitution here, such as the E♭min chord I suggested earlier, if you're having trouble making the stretch, but as one of the points of this track is to do a bit of exploring, I'd advise you to try to manage the full version. It's an interesting chord, particularly because of its construction, as it's partially made up purely from successive perfect fourths. Getting used to the sounds of chords like this one improves your ear training no end and will enable you to identify different harmonies. If you plan to take jazz playing any further, you'll soon come across specific chord constructions like this one, based around fourths.

The second verse bar, meanwhile, doesn't feature any new types of chord, but look at the mixture of simple harmony in the first two chords and the more jazzy-sounding G♭maj7 in the third. (Note the dissonant minor-second interval in the right hand between F and G♭.)

The second verse bar's counterpart, the fourth, is quite different in harmonic approach. Again, no new types of chord are used, but the voicing used between both hands is worth looking at. On both the A♭min7 and the B♭min7, the right hand makes no reference to either chord's tonic note; the left hand – along with the bass player – pins both of these chords down to root position with an A♭ and B♭ respectively. (Remember, it's the very bottom note of a chord that determines its position.)

The second verse is very similar to the first, but check out the voicings used; there are many subtle changes here and there, and the inversions used are often higher, with the top notes ascending and descending to give a hint of a theme.

Pedalling

A few general suggestions in this department. For a start, using the pedal on the sustained chords in the verse section (such as in bars 10, 12, etc) requires quick changes if the chords are not to blur together. As before, keep working on bringing the pedal up as you play the next chord. Think of it as being one simultaneous motion and you'll soon get it.

In sections where the pedal is to be used over a similar passage, the direction *simile* means you should keep pedalling in the same way over the following bars. When further pedal markings are given, disregard the *simile* marking from that point on, until it's indicated again.

Bridge

The most interesting parts of this bridge section, which links the two verses, are the rhythmic feature in the last bar and the use of voicings to keep the top notes of all the chords within a very small area.

When all the instruments in a group play a rhythmic feature such as the one in the final bar of the bridge, they are known as *stops*. The ones here should all be played in a short, marked style, so all of them have been marked staccato, with the last three given additional accents.

More On Voicing

We've seen several times in earlier tracks how an approach to voicing a sequence of chords can vary depending on what you want to do. If the part is exposed and needs to play a prominent role, you can voice chords so that the top notes play a theme, or move in a tuneful way. Likewise, where chords need to be more subtle, they can be voiced in such a way that the physical (and tonal) movement is as small as possible.

The latter is the case in this bridge section, and looking at the arrangement of chords in the first six bars, you can see that the top notes remain the same for many of them, despite the fact that there are many different chords used. As you should know by now, this is due to the use of inversions. As there are no new types of chord used here, I won't go into a detailed blow-by-blow account of each one; instead, it's up to you to look at each of them and see and hear how it's constructed.

Middle-eight

In fact, this section is 17 bars long, but as I said earlier, a middle-eight doesn't necessarily have to conform to an eight-bar length. It's preceded by an eight-bar passage played by just bass and drums, which sets the tone for the middle-eight proper.

Let's consider the make-up of this middle-eight. It starts off low-key, then builds and ends by using the same kind of stops that were played at the end of the bridge.

The way in which the chords are constructed here reflects their use. The whole section uses essentially the same three chords – E♭min7, B♭min7 and A♭min7 – in an identical order, so in order to bring some colour and interest to the part there are several subtly different versions of the same chords presented here. Look at the way in which the chords build in pitch as the section builds and grows dynamically, leading up to the stops at the end.

Summary

Although two more backing tracks follow (to be used with the section on soloing and improvisation), this part of the book – dealing with the in-depth analysis of keyboard parts – now comes to an end. The idea behind working with these backing tracks is hopefully to give you some insight, and help, in making up your own parts within various playing situations.

Above all, remember that you're making music from the heart, and with this in mind you should allow yourself to be guided by musical ideals. We all need to work things out sometimes by mechanical means, but never lose sight of one fact: the technology is there only to help you make music.

9 FURTHER PLAYING TIPS

'Music is your own experience, your own thoughts, your wisdom.' – *Charlie Parker*

Improvisation

To many non-musicians, the ability to sit down at an instrument and just make up something on the spot seems an almost fantastic impossibility. Yet to acquire some ability in improvisation is a lot less daunting than you might think.

When you talk, for instance, you don't plan each word of every sentence; you subconsciously map out the general direction of your conversation and, from the array of words in your vocabulary, you make a selection to use. Improvising and soloing are not dissimilar in this respect; you already have a lot of information in your head – probably more than you realise – about different keys, chords and scales, and you can use this knowledge – combined with a sense of general musical direction – to become more proficient at improvising than you might believe.

There are two distinct issues here. The first, improvisation, describes the basic skill of making it up as you go along, for want of a better expression. It also, more commonly, refers to a player's ability to sit down at an instrument and compose something to play from scratch.

The second issue, soloing, is something of which most of you will have heard or had experience – namely, improvising within a passage of a song or piece of music, where you take over the main point of musical interest. We'll be taking a more detailed look at soloing in this chapter, partly because it's something that you're more likely to need to do, and also because it gives you a starting point for more general improvisation at a later point.

Soloing

You've all heard solos on well-known recordings, and you'll no doubt know how sometimes they can be as important as great lyrics or a memorable chorus. The thing is, how do you come up with something like that? Is it down to natural musical ability, or is it a skill that can be learnt?

Well, this is something of a moot point, because out of a selection of the best solos ever, the playing skills and musical abilities of the performers will vary enormously.

Stunning solos can sometimes be composed of only a few notes, so don't think that advanced technical ability is a must-have. Think back to what I said many chapters ago about there being nothing wrong with a simple yet effective playing style. It's the ability to *think* of something that counts, and then to allow your technique to carry out your ideas as best it can.

This, in time, can lead you to start thinking of things which are some way above your technical ability, which is good; as well as a spur to keep you working on your technique, it's a sign that you're doing things the right way around. You shouldn't allow your technical limitations to dictate too much of what you play. If you get into the habit of doing this, you'll end up just playing things that are comfortable.

However, you do need some basic musical knowledge as a starting point. As you take in more information, you'll find yourself using it in your playing and coming up with your own original ideas.

So, let's pitch in to a musical scenario and imagine you're playing a song that has a keyboard solo in it. First off, you need to have a framework – a basis on which to start. No matter what style of music you're playing, there will always be some bits of primary information that will help you, as follows.

- The first, and most obvious, thing to be aware of is the length of the solo passage. Within a typical pop song, this can be anything from 4–16 bars.

- Next, you need to know the key signature and sequence of chords over which you'll be soloing; your solo has to fit around them. Look at the harmonic movement of these chords – do they stay the same or change during the solo passage? If they move around a bit, your solo will need to fit in with the new chords.

- You'll also need to know the type of time signature and the tempo.

Finding Notes That Fit

Without much doubt, the main difficulty that most people face when beginning to solo is in finding the right kind of notes to play. Rhythm is just as much a part of musicality as pitch, of course, but while you can tap or clap a rhythm using your hands, getting started with the right kind of notation can seem to be a bit of a minefield. However, it's not as difficult as you might think; you just need a combination of ideas and a bit of music theory to help you put them into practice. The ideas can be developed as you gain proficiency (and studying other soloists can be a major help here), while music theory can be studied up to an extremely detailed level, although understanding the basic principles is enough to get you started.

Using Backing Track 6

We're going to use two backing tracks to help us here, both featuring an interesting yet straightforward progression of chords. While it's of great importance to make the notes of the solo fit over the chords, the more

simple the harmony, the more concentration you can spare on the solo.

Before looking at anything else, just play the first track, Backing Track 6 (Track 27), right through and hum along. Try not to think of a format or rhythmic approach. Once you've done this a few times, you might find you've noticed something: without being aware of any of the technical details of the track, you've (hopefully) found in your head some notes that fit against the chords underneath. Listen to it a few more times and you might start to develop some ideas of a tune or find a few notes in sequence that sound good.

There's a lot more to soloing than this, of course, but hopefully this exercise has shown you that, left to your own devices, you can come up with at least *something*. At this stage, your embryonic solo will need development, but it's enough to demonstrate that the essence of finding ideas in your mind isn't as hard as it might seem...

Now listen to the track again and take a look at the chord sequence used in Backing Track 6, Dmaj to Dmin7:

 Track 27

Tempo: ♩ = 68

D major | D minor

If you wanted to find notes that fitted over this sequence, the obvious starting point would be to take them from the chords themselves. As a D major chord is made up from the notes D, F♯ and A, you can play any of these notes against the chord and they will fit. Likewise, the notes that make up a Dmin7 chord – D, F, A and C – will all fit against the parent chord.

While this approach might seem extremely basic, it's nevertheless a useful exercise to play the track and just get used to playing these notes against the relevant chords. Experiment by playing the notes in different orders and rhythms.

While it's technically possible to construct a solo using only this handful of notes, think back to when you hummed against the track: you almost certainly used other notes as well. You thought of notes that sounded close to the notes in the key chords, that related to them in some way, and in doing so you made a subconscious reference to a scale.

Now repeat the above experiment, but this time play any of the notes from a D major scale over the D major

chord and any of the notes from a pure D minor scale over the Dmin7 chord. Even though you obviously couldn't play a solo quite like that, you now have a structure from which to choose your notes. Some notes will sound better than others in this context, for reasons we'll come to in a moment. Before we do, though, play the track through a few more times and try to mix the notes up a bit, using different note lengths.

While this approach to finding notes for your solo is somewhat technical, it's still a good starting point to finding your way around the whole idea. It also creates a framework, a format for your brain to use and develop ideas.

Hum against the track again, and this time try to identify the notes you're humming. Hear which ones you use more instinctively against each of the two chords and, equally importantly, at which part of each bar you like the sound of certain notes.

Although this example uses only two chords, you can use the same principle with any chord as a starting point by finding the scale to which the chord refers and using the notes it contains. This is a great way of familiarising yourself with some of the notes that will fit a given chord. Whole books are devoted to the detailed analysis of soloing, but here, using the opening two chords as a reference, I want to touch briefly on a few general musical implications.

Soloing In General

You'll have heard that, just by playing the notes of the key chord, the whole thing sounds OK – it fits, musically – but there's no sense of musical direction or dynamics. Likewise, when you add in other notes from the scale, some notes sound good while others don't. This is where rhythmic emphasis and the mixture of sweet and dissonant harmonies come again into play.

For an example, play a D major triad in your left hand. Now play a D major scale in your right and replay the D

major chord with each note. The notes in the key chord – D, F♯ and A – all sound sweet, but the notes in between – E, G, B and C♯ – don't.

When soloing over chord changes, you need to be aware that playing notes outside the key chord (in this case, the E, G, B and C♯ against the D major) can clash and sound a bit odd if they are emphasised *on the beat*. At this stage, try to avoid playing long sustained notes from outside the key chord on the beat as they will highlight the dissonance present. Instead, try using these notes from outside the key chord to join up the spaces in between the onbeat harmonic notes. Notes that are used in this way, to fill in the gaps between harmonic notes, are known as *passing notes*. In the illustration below, the second, sixth and eighth notes of the first bar (right hand) are all examples of passing notes, and all are off the beat:

Using The Pentatonic Scale

We had a quick look at the pentatonic scale in an earlier chapter. To recap briefly, it's made up from five notes – the tonic, second, third, fifth and sixth – leaving a clean-sounding series of notes. Pentatonic scales are used by

many players as basic tools for finding solo notation, and are popular because of their harmonically sweet sound.

Within the verse section of Backing Track 6, try using the pentatonic versions of D major and D minor to form your notation:

D major pentatonic scale

D minor pentatonic scale

It's useful to hear the effect of a pentatonic scale, but remember that it's only a major or minor scale with a couple of notes left out. While it can sometimes be helpful to use a pentatonic scale as a basis for a selection of notes to use, if you rely on it – or, indeed, on any other scale – you're in danger of falling into the habit of playing by numbers. Retain the information contained within and the sounds produced by different scales, but view them as pots of knowledge to be dipped into. Try to retain the characteristic sounds of each different type of scale in your head and think how each could be used in various solo situations.

Rhythmic Ideas

A solo needs to have phrasing and rhythmic ideas to be convincing. When you hummed along to Backing Track 6, you didn't just hum notes of equal length all the way through, did you? Instead, you naturally mixed up the rhythm to give the solo variation. In a solo, interest is maintained by using a mixture of different note lengths and phrasing to give it contour and shape. Rhythmic ideas, just like notation, vary enormously depending upon the genre of music being played and the length of the solo in question. To explore this area further, we need to take a look at the whole area of rhythm using another backing track.

Backing Track 7

♩ = 68   **Verse section (do not solo over)**

Track 28

| D major | D minor | D major | D minor |

| D major | D minor | D major | D minor |

Solo section

| D major | B♭ major | D major | B♭ major |

| D major | B♭ major | D major | B♭ major |

Verse and solo section repeat

70

Using Backing Track 7

This backing track has got sections, referred to here as the verse and solo sections. Listen to the verse part, and when it reaches the solo section, before you do anything else, just listen to it and remember the things I told you to look out for earlier, ie:

- The length of the solo passage (eight bars here);

- The sequence of chords that you'll be soloing over (D major to B♭ major, a sequence that stays in place here during the length of the solo);

- The time signature and the tempo (here, 4/4 and medium-paced).

Over this second eight-bar length, your solo will be the main focus of interest, so it needs to tell a story; in other words, it needs to have a beginning, a middle and an end. It must also represent the direction of the music, fitting the part of the track in which it's played. Backing Track 7 has only two sections, verse and solo, but you can still hear quite clearly how the music underneath the solo section is more exciting and dominant. Therefore your solo can't start with a whimper; it has to make a positive, decisive opening statement.

At some stage during the eight bars, try to reach a peak – a musical high point – in your playing, and as the track goes back to the quieter, more sensitive verse, look for a way to tone down your the solo toward the end.

This might sound like a lot of instruction to take in at once, but if you hum your way through the track before you play anything you'll find it's not as hard as you might think to fall into this kind of thinking – structuring a solo passage around a beginning, middle and end. The most effective ways of building excitement in a solo are often the obvious ones:

- Ascending in pitch;

- Increasing in volume;

- Quickening the rhythmic pace.

Likewise, the opposite applies for bringing things back down and subduing the mood.

Try starting the solo with something melodic. Think about using a sequence of relatively few notes for the first four bars, then build the solo using these melodic ideas and the suggestions noted above for increasing excitement and bringing the mood down at the end.

A Few Tips

- When playing slower, more melodic ideas, instead of playing them all on the beat, vary them rhythmically. Try mixing up note lengths, and don't be afraid to use a bit of syncopation here and there. It'll help to maintain interest.

- You'll find that the ideas that work best often lend themselves to repetition. Sometimes, just one good feature – focusing on either rhythm or notation – can be used a basis for a complete solo section.

- Look for notes that will fit over more than one chord in a solo section. For instance, D, G and A can be found in the keys of both D major and B♭ major (and are therefore handy for soloing over Backing Track 7). The notes will have a different quality over each chord, but this can be an advantage.

- Try to start the solo using notes that are closely related to the chords beneath them. The start of a solo is a statement, and a simple, solid beginning makes it easier for the listener to get into what you're doing.

- A solo is a performance, so stay focused on it – don't lose your sense of direction. Even if you're not sure it's working out, stay with it to the end. You'll never improve if you don't follow through your ideas.

- Likewise, if a specific idea or approach hasn't worked, don't dump it completely; you might find that it works in another solo situation.

- When playing faster lines, again try to think of your musical direction. Don't just recite a selection of major and minor scales; instead, use parts of scales – maybe three or four notes at a time – to help you put your ideas into practice.

- Breaking up a solo into two halves, or even smaller divisions, can really help when you're trying to get a form together. Doing this will not only help you get an overall idea of where you're going, musically, but also help you phrase the solo. Remember to let the music *breathe*. A long, uninterrupted series of notes leaves most people cold.

- Solos come in all shapes and sizes. Nevertheless, you should always remember – whatever the length of your solo – that it should have a start, a middle and an end.

Modes

I can't leave the subject of soloing and improvising without touching on the concept of modes. I don't actually think you need to know much about them for now; while I'm a firm believer in acquiring as much knowledge as possible, understanding modes is essentially all about re-ordering knowledge and information that you should have already.

Basically, a mode is just a scale that starts from a point other than the tonic. For example, below is a textbook C major scale:

C major scale

Now, if we keep the key signature exactly the same – no sharps or flats in this instance – but start the scale not on C but on D, we have created a mode, in this case one that's known as the *Dorian*:

C Dorian mode

If you want to look deeper into the subject of modes, suitable reference books can be obtained from most music shops. You might find them to be a useful basis for studying improvisation and soloing at a later stage in your playing, but at this stage your time would be better spent experimenting. Take a few scales and try starting them on different notes – essentially, you're using modes.

Rather than spending a lot of time learning all the different modes and their names right now, I'd suggest persevering with humming along ideas of your own, then listening to and identifying the notes you're humming. Modes make more sense when you've established a good sense of major and minor keys and chords, but even then there's no substitute for using and developing your ears.

10 TIPS FOR PERFORMING AND RECORDING

'What an audience wants is an experience, a living experience, and that's why the concert will always exist; the moment of creation, the moment the artist gets on stage and actually makes that performance.'
– *Yehudi Menuhin*

Nerves

All performers worth their salt – even the very best – get excited before going onstage. When they get out there, though, their minds turn to the task that lies ahead of them and they *focus*. This doesn't mean that the sense of excitement then disappears, but it does mean that they can control it and deal with it by concentrating on the job in hand, which is to give a *performance*. Come what may, they will play their instruments to the best of their abilities, and once they're onstage, that's all they'll think about. Sure, mistakes will happen sometimes, but that's occupying such a small space in their minds that the chances of it happening are small. Instead, they're focused on playing a piece of music from start to end, and that's it.

So, one of the golden rules about performing live is that you should never be afraid to make a mistake. That might seem like pretty crazy advice, but it's not as daft as it sounds. When I say 'never be afraid', I mean that you shouldn't waste time *worrying* about making a mistake; instead, accept that there will simply be times when you'll fluff a passage or play bum notes – even the greatest players do. Of course, the more you practise and the better prepared you are, the less likely you are to drop a note, but what distinguishes a good performer from a bad one in this respect is how they deal with it when it happens onstage.

When you do have a problem in a performing situation (and we're talking about maybe a few wrong notes or a wrong chord here), it's easy to lose your composure. This is partially born out of a subconscious need to acknowledge to the audience that you've made a mistake, and yet this is the very worst thing you can do, mainly because very few people will probably have noticed! When you practise a piece or a song endlessly, you familiarise yourself with it to a far greater extent than anyone in the audience will know it, so it often takes quite a major bodge for anyone to recognise an error, and even then your only thought has to be *to carry on as if nothing has happened*. If your overall performance is still good, people usually forget mistakes very quickly.

It's also a fact of life that some people feel more comfortable while performing than others. This doesn't necessarily spring from a natural tendency to be an exhibitionist, but is instead attributable to the confidence they have in their own abilities, which is a rather different thing. In this area of performing, there's no substitute to having a good physical relationship with your instrument, which you'll have developed through the process of getting really comfortable with new techniques, getting your form right and not rushing through new areas.

So don't take the attitude that nerves are things to be conquered; instead, make use of them. Take advantage of the extra edge they give you onstage, and adjust your mental attitude toward not worrying too much about mistakes. Provided that you've prepared yourself as much as you can (and only you can know whether or not you have), you should start to develop the ability to perform to your maximum ability, which is all part of stagecraft in general.

Coping With Recording

Studio recording can bring its own set of issues. In some ways, playing onstage can seem easier, because you have more leeway to make mistakes. Even if it's noticed, the audience's concentration will shift onto the next part of the performance. In a recording environment, however, what you play will be analysed more carefully and errors will be more noticeable. Some players enjoy the extra pressure that this can bring, but you should play it just as you would onstage: give a performance.

In these days of computer-based recording, it's pretty easy – particularly when recording via MIDI – to correct even quite heinous musical wrongdoings. You could even take things further and negate the need to play anything at all by instead programming the keyboard part directly from the computer. What this can't do, though, is give the recording its most important part: a human element. Sure, the more precise you are, the better, but it shouldn't be at the expense of putting in a musical performance.

Even if you're recording the old-fashioned way, using tape, there is still the possibility of inserting an *overdub* by *dropping* or *punching in* to record over just part of a take, which involves putting whatever multitrack tape-recording machine you're using into Record mode while the track is playing. This technique allows you to keep the good bits of a take while recording over something that needs correcting (provided that there's space) and dropping or punching out again. While using tape is less common than it used to be, it's still perfectly feasible to repair parts this way, if it's done with a reasonable degree of care.

So don't think you necessarily have to get all of a recording right in one go. You should always aim toward that, but, as I said earlier, don't be afraid to make – or even think about making – a mistake; if need be, you can either correct it later or do another take.

One way to become more comfortable with recording is to do more of it. If you rehearse with a band, get into the habit of recording your practice sessions. If you spend more time playing at home, get a sequencing package for your computer and get used to recording that way. Also, as always, you should listen to as many different bands and artists as possible; it's an interesting exercise to try to hear the difference between a great live take and a programmed one...

Sightreading

Oh dear! If there's one thing that can make otherwise hardboiled musicians tremble at the knees, it's the prospect of having to sightread. This is a real shame, because an ability to sightread gives you the facility to experience and appreciate music you might otherwise never play.

Even so, many people look on sightreading as being a straightforward technical exercise, which is incorrect; it requires as much musicianship and intuition as any other aspect of performance. Good players who sightread well are sometimes accused by others of 'playing by numbers', almost as if good reading ability somehow presses a Bypass button in the musicianship department. Put bluntly, however, this is total crap; being able to sightread opens a door to a whole host of musical experiences. And if you're hoping to earn any money from your playing, you might well be expected at some stage to do a bit of sightreading.

While anyone can suggest techniques for improving sightreading, everyone has their own way of dealing with it, so here I'm just going to outline a few basic suggestions which I think might help. Beyond that, there's no real secret to it; it's just a matter of practising.

Being Put On The Spot

The worst possible scenario for anyone lacking confidence in their sightreading is being put on the spot, most commonly onstage. It's easy to forget when you're in this kind of situation that, in essence, you still need to give a performance. Of course, the more detail you can recognise, take in and play, the better, but the most crucial thing is to capture the *spirit* of the music. Therefore, sightreading becomes not just a technical exercise, in terms of reading the part, but a musical one where you use your ear, intuition and experience (where possible) to control the situation.

Nevertheless, you should always start by having a quick look through the part you're about to play, if possible. It's actually possible to take in a lot of information within a few seconds. Here are a few things to look out for:

- Note how long the piece lasts. Make sure you can find the end and that it looks complete – ie there aren't any hidden passages likely to spring out at you.

- What kind of piece is it? If it's a pop song, it may well have a simple structure centred around verse, chorus and middle-eight sections, which will often be either 8, 12 or 16 bars long. By relaxing and trying to feel the natural length of each of these sections, you can usually tell where it might go next.

- Note the tempo and the time and key signatures of the piece, as well as the type of notation used. A lot of songs start and end in one key, so think about what the relative minor or major key might be for the piece and look out for it cropping up. Also, try to make a note of the dynamic markings, as this will help you to start forming an idea of the piece in your mind.

- Most pop songs use a fairly limited selection of chords and similar rhythmic patterns, so keep your eyes peeled for areas of repetition. This kind of ability can allow you to scan through parts quickly.

- Likewise, look for areas that might cause problems. If the piece as a whole looks fairly manageable, use whatever time you have to focus on these problem areas.

Even taking all of these precautions, however, there will often be an unexpected surprise lurking ahead – a chord you might not expect, or a difficult-looking riff. This is where there really is no substitute for practice and experience. Even the most accomplished readers come across awkward sections at some stage, and when this happens it's up to you to use your musical instinct to help you out. Remember, it's the *spirit* of the part that needs to come across; sometimes you can get away with not playing all the notes in a certain chord or studiously playing all the smaller nuances of a part. As long as you keep going and maintain the tempo and basic feel of the piece, you should minimise problem areas.

The other valuable method of helping to cope with this is perhaps the golden rule when it comes to sightreading: *look ahead*.

Summary

The advice in this chapter will hopefully help you to develop a good overall approach to sightreading on the spot, but as far as your general sightreading ability is concerned, the more you do it, the better you'll be. This is something that applies to your overall musical ability too, of course, but it's even more true of sightreading; you really do need to practise it with a view to identifying notes and rhythms quickly. The time you spend at home, without pressure, just enjoying looking through new books of pieces and songs will be the main factor in developing your sightreading skills.

11 TIPS AND WORKOUTS

'There are a million things in music I know nothing about. I just want to narrow down that figure.' – *André Previn*

'For me, I think the only danger is being too much in love with playing. The *music* is the most important thing, and the [guitar] is only the instrument' – *Jerry Garcia*

This chapter gives a few tips, suggestions and workouts to get you thinking about your playing.

Hand Stretch

Contrary to what many people think, there's no need to have massive paws in order to play the piano. Yes, it's pretty helpful to be able to stretch an octave between thumb and little finger, but most adults can manage that (although an extra note or two above this can be helpful). What counts is how much strength and independence you have *within* that stretch. Developing this will help you to play more substantial chords, as well as increasing your

general dexterity and nimbleness. Backing Track 5 brought up the first big (right-hand) chord in this book:

It's actually not that big a chord. The difficulty lies in playing it using carefully gauged arm weight, not just plonking it down. To get your fingers used to the shape and size of this chord, play it as an arpeggio, thus:

Play it over and over as an arpeggiated figure, using different rhythms, as described in Chapter 1. Make sure you play it as legato as possible, with a smooth transition between each note. Then, when it starts to feel a bit easier, start holding on a few of the notes, like this:

Then try playing them all staccato:

All of these methods will (hopefully) even out the awkward bits in the chord. I don't want you to stop there, though; one of the main weaknesses can be between the fourth and fifth fingers, so to give these digits a bit of a workout, add a D♭ to the chord below, like this:

Use the same techniques as described on the previous page: arpeggiate the chord in alternate rhythms, first holding on to each note in sequence and then playing it staccato. Any chord that uses all five fingers like this – such as a straight major, minor or seventh chord – with the key note added at the top (like the chord at the top of the next column) helps to develop strength in the weaker fingers:

Developing Hand Independence

A high degree of independence between your hands is a very valuable commodity to have. In certain situations, it can be difficult to play different rhythms in the left hand and right hand, or to get each hand playing at a different dynamic level, but you'll also find that developing hand independence is a pretty indispensable tool when it comes to everyday playing. To help you get started, here are a few suggestions.

Start off by taking a few bars of a straightforward eighth-note triplet figure, firstly played in the right hand only, as shown here:

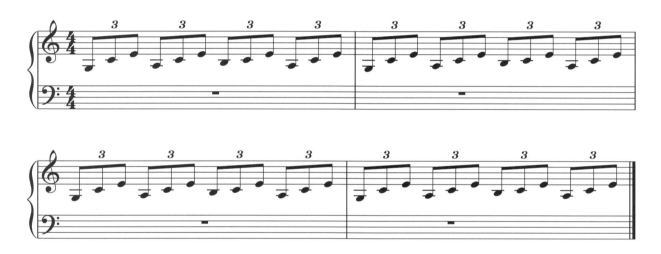

Then play the first note of each group of three in the left hand. Keep playing legato so that the change to the next note is as smooth as possible:

Now play the first two notes in the left hand:

In a 16th-note situation, develop this idea further by mixing up rhythms between the left and right hands. Concentrate primarily on getting the order of notes in each hand comfortable before playing it at any sort of tempo:

A further development is to syncopate the rhythm:

Hand independence isn't just concerned with rhythm, though. It's very easy to get into a habit of playing only certain things with each hand – for instance, the right hand tends to do most of the tunes and chordal work while the left hand can, over time, become under-developed. It's therefore a good idea to reverse roles sometimes and use the left hand to play a theme with the right hand accompanying it, like this:

100 bpm

It's a simple eight-bar piece, but the object is to play the left hand at a louder level than the right. Therefore the right hand is marked *p* (quietly) and the left is marked *mf* (moderately loudly). This kind of playing can be harder than you might think…

Contrary-Motion Scale

This kind of scale is particularly useful in that, while it's based around a normal major or minor, it encourages you to break out of conventional playing patterns, which can become something of a habit. Think about it – you normally play scales with both hands going in the same direction and playing the same notes. However, a contrary-motion scale – as its name implies – is characterised by one hand playing an ascending version of a scale while the other plays a descending version. Your hands therefore move in opposite (contrary) directions to each other, like this:

C major contrary-motion scale

Play the scale over at least two octaves and, in time, in each key and variation.

Chromatic Scale

We've touched on the basic definition of chromatics, in that a chromatic series of notes is one where each note is a semitone away from its neighbour (in other words, they're directly adjacent to each other, separated by only a semitone). The principle behind the chromatic scale is pretty easy to understand: unlike major or minor scales, which are made up from varying patterns of whole tones and semitones, the chromatic scale is formed using every available note within the 12-tone scale. Therefore, taking the note of C as a starting point, a chromatic scale looks like this:

Chromatic scale

While it doesn't really matter, in terms of notes, where you start and end the scale (as a chromatic scale cannot, by definition, have a key signature), the fingering can vary, depending on which note you start playing. And, of course, you can also play a chromatic scale in contrary motion.

Major-Seventh And Minor-Seventh Inverted Arpeggios

By now you should be aware of what major-seventh and minor-seventh chords and arpeggios are, and you should be familiar with the fact that they can be inverted, just like any other chord or arpeggio. What follows are a few suggestions for using both major- and minor-seventh chords which you'll find useful, both as warm-up exercises and as something to have under your belt that you can later use in solo sections.

Take this next exercise as an example, based around the key of A major. It's based around a major-seventh chord on the way up but an A minor-seventh chord on the way down:

Dexterity

There are many books out there packed with exercises designed to improve dexterity and finger stretch. One of the foremost teachers of playing technique (and also an eminent composer of the period) was Carl Czerny, an ex-pupil of Beethoven's who published several books on the subject in the 19th century. Among Czerny's own pupils, of course, was the legendary Franz Liszt, undoubtedly one of the greatest, most spectacular pianists ever, so it appears that Czerny knew what he was talking about! His book of exercises *The School Of Velocity* is a particularly well-respected tutor in the music world, containing exercises designed to develop technique and playing strength. However, there are provisos to be aware of with this type of book:

1   Never forget that playing the keyboard is a two-handed business. Don't be tempted to learn the more difficult examples only in your right hand, thinking that you'll never need to have that degree of technical ability in your left.

2   Don't get lost in playing endless repetitions. At the end of the day, exercises are there to help you put into practice the things in your mind; they're not pieces of music in themselves. Also, *play* them each time you do them; don't just hammer up and down the keyboard without thinking.

3   You'll find yourself getting tired quite quickly with some exercises, so don't overdo it. If you feel any twinges underneath the forearm (where you would buckle a watch), stop straight away.

4   Above all – and I really can't stress this enough – you must practise exercises *slowly*. You'll never make any real progress unless you do. Bring each exercise up to tempo over a period of time, but still practise it slowly even when you've reached that stage.

12 TURNING PROFESSIONAL

'Music – what a beautiful art, but what a wretched profession.' – *Georges Bizet*

'My sole inspiration is a telephone call from a producer.' – *Cole Porter*

'I don't know anything about music. In my line you don't have to.' – *Elvis Presley*

At some stage along the musical path, many people think about the idea of becoming a professional musician, and certainly some will be able to work themselves into a money-earning position. But as for a career as a full time musician… Well, I don't want to come over all negative, but it's a lot easier to earn a bit of money from music than to make a living from it. It's easy to get carried away after having made a few quid from gigging, and my advice would be, for most people, to keep your music as a pleasurable, part-time activity. Regard any income you derive from it as a supplement to your everyday profession.

The music industry can portray an unrepresentative image of lifestyle and expectations – at least for the majority of working musicians. Sure, a guy playing onstage with Sting is a professional musician, but then so is someone playing in the house band at Butlins for £35 a night. The reality can be somewhat different from the seemingly glamorous world presented by the media.

Additionally, relatively few musicians I know – including top session players – have earned what could be described as a good living year in, year out. They might have had good periods, but once the tour has ended or the album's been recorded, there are often long periods of inactivity, which translates as unemployment.

Further down the scale, for a freelance player, a regular gig can be a rarity, and in any case is seldom enough to get by. The fact is that simply being a paid musician is bloody hard work, and it can be incredibly stressful. As a career move, I'd hardly recommend it.

On the other hand, there are many good points to consider, some of which relate to any self-employed business. For instance, you decide whether or not you want to accept work (if you're lucky enough to be able to afford that luxury), and there's often a lot of free time involved – usually more than you'd like there to be! Crucially, though, like any other self-employed person, how well you get on isn't just down to how well you play or how much you know; it's down to how good a businessperson you are.

The phone isn't just going to ring; if you want to find work, you need to put yourself about.

Playing And/Or Composing

There are two paths to be taken in this business. One is being a 'normal' earning musician – doing gigs, a bit of teaching, recording or whatever other sidelines you can find. You can do this right from the bottom level (playing in pubs and clubs) up to the higher echelons (touring and recording with signed artists). While you're unlikely to become rich this way, by being flexible and having a few sources of income you'll be giving yourself the best chance of earning a decent living.

The second path – which often encompasses a bit of the first as well – is to compose your own music and sell it. You could do this as a member of a group, as a solo artist or simply as a writer whose material is performed by other artists. If you can make it work, this kind of endeavour can launch you into an area of the business that can be highly lucrative. Look at most of the wealthy artists in the music business and they have all been, either individually or jointly, composers or songwriters.

The reason why there's so much money involved in this area of the music business is mainly because of the potential revenue within music publishing. Not in the paperback sense, you understand; in the music world, the word *publishing* refers to the royalties paid to a composer whenever his or her material is broadcast. At best, a hit song can earn a fortune for the writer. Lower down the scale, though, there are other opportunities, such as library-music or soundtrack work, areas in which many professional musicians manage to find work.

Being A Working Musician

So, looking at the first option, of being a basic earning musician without any particular ambition to go to the top of the scale, how good do you need to be? Straight away, we enter the paradoxic nature of the music business. As I explained earlier, merely being a good player doesn't necessarily translate into lots of work. It's that all-round situation again in which playing ability plays a large (although by no means exclusive) part. I would sum up the most important areas as follows:

Be A Good Person To Work With
This is somewhat obvious, maybe, but an ability to mix and get on with fellow musicians is a prerequisite. Working in a gigging or recording environment often means spending long periods travelling or hanging around. There's no need to be the life and soul of the party, just do the basic things right: be on time, be reliable and be easy to work with.

Have Reasonable Equipment And Make Sure You Know How It Works
We'll see in later chapters, you don't need to spend a lot of money to get a good sound, provided that you can get the most out of what you've got. For starters, you'll need at least a couple of keyboards or rack units and, ideally, a small desk and keyboard amp. Keep them in good working order and invest in some flightcases to protect your gear in transit. A few gigs' worth of chucking electronic gear in and out of vans and you'll soon see the wisdom of protecting it.

Have Your Own Transport
If you don't drive, you'll need to learn. Gigging invariably involves having to get to inaccessible places at unsociable hours.

Put Yourself About
Making contact with others in the business, either through direct promotional means or (usually better) through introductions from fellow colleagues, is your lifeblood. If no one knows you're there, they can't ask you to do anything.

Getting to know people can initially be a bit of a daunting task. In this respect, a local music scene can be the easiest way to start to get around. Look for advertisements placed in local music shops, rehearsal rooms and newspapers by covers bands looking for keyboard players. (Lots of free-ads papers also run adverts like these.) Get to know the people who run the local rehearsal rooms and recording studios. Nothing may come of your efforts for a while, but your name will soon get around if you work on making yourself known. If you can play solo, approach a few restaurants or bars that stage live music.

When you've found a few working situations, don't stop there. Hopefully, the grapevine will yield a few calls from people requiring your talents, but don't rely on this. Keep searching and maximising your chances of obtaining work.

Look Presentable
Like it or not, the way you look will have a direct bearing on the kind of work you're likely to end up doing. If you want to be a working musician, the likely venues at which you'll be performing in – such as clubs and function rooms – will mean that you can't be too outlandish in your appearance. You've got to look right for the kind of work you want to get, and for the purposes of this particular example, you'll need to project a more restrained image than you might prefer.

That said, however, adopting a trendy and arty look can be a definite plus in certain areas.

Moving Up The Scale
If you want to be a bit more ambitious and try to get session work playing for name artists, this requires a somewhat different approach. Most of this kind of work comes from word of mouth, so the wider your circle of musician friends, the better. When you enter this more elevated area of the business, factors such as image and equipment become even more important; you've got to look as if you could realistically be in a band that goes onstage and performs at big venues – and this applies not only to your appearance but also to your confidence in performing in such a situation. Again, playing ability isn't necessarily the sole criterion at work here; many session players are good, solid musicians who perform and move around well onstage.

Aside from your own contacts, you might want to approach agents who fix musicians for bigger name artists. You can sometimes find lists of these in media reference books in your local library. Remember that your presentation must reflect the kind of work you're going for, and this means you'll need to get a really good professional picture taken, along with – ideally – a CV or brochure and a quality CD that shows off your playing abilities. And even then, don't expect to have a high rate of reply; you might well get none.

Composing Music
Selling your own music can be one of the most satisfying experiences in the business. It can also be one of the most frustrating, as not only are openings hard to come by but you also face a lot of competition from other groups or individual writers.

For many people, writing outside a group situation is likely to be more applicable, so I'll concentrate on giving advice to anyone who wants to compose either on their own or maybe with a co-writer.

Your first job is to look at the genres open to you – songs or instrumentals – and decide which suits you best, then condense this list further and decide on specific areas. For instance, looking at songs first of all, many writers focus on composing pop tunes with a view to them being taken up by artists who don't write their own material. If successful, this can be a particularly lucrative area, although very competitive. The key to successful writing is in supplying the right material for a particular genre, so if this is where you want to earn your cash, study the musical area you want to write for and hear how sounds and production styles work in conjunction with that genre of music.

Recording

When you have the bare bones of what you think might be a promising track, record a version at home first of all (and if you're serious about this, you'll have invested in a reasonable home recording setup – which, again, doesn't have to be expensive) and hone it until you have a version that you think works. If you can't sing it yourself, pay a session vocalist to perform it for you. Remember, you're essentially recording a demo here, but if you think it's worth it, you might want to record it in a higher-quality studio than your own to give it that extra bit of polish that might get you noticed. Again, however, time is often the critical requirement in recording, and if you can't afford enough hours in a better studio, you're often better off recording your material at home.

Publishers

Once you have the completed CD in your hand, the people you really need to contact are those music publishers who have influence and clout in the industry. You can easily find out who these are by looking at the credits section on any big-name CD. The question then is, will they take you seriously?

This is unfortunately where you're on your own, and your success in this area is largely down to how good at business you are. All I will say is this: If a publisher hears a CD full of material he thinks could be a hit for someone, he'll take an interest in it. He'd be a fool not to. Getting it to him, and being taken seriously, is the hurdle you have to overcome. As is so often the case, persistence is the key. Keep sending out new recordings, always improving your material and learning new techniques and avenues of distribution. It can take many, many rejections or non-replies before you're successful in placing material you've composed. Many give up without any success at all.

Instrumental Music

Instrumental music has a rather wider market than vocal music. In addition to film, TV, advertising and library music, the world of multimedia opens up many new doors, such as the computer-game industry. In this field, the quality of music produced has increased substantially in recent years, and again there is a lot of competition between fellow composers. (Many good games musicians are often out of work.)

Library music, meanwhile, is usually commissioned directly from specialist publishers, and your (by now well-used) media reference book will tell you who they are. Again, you need to find the right kind of sound to succeed with library music – it's often used behind commercials or within TV programmes created with only a small budget for music. Watch satellite daytime channels for examples of shows that use this kind of material. You'll find that this type of music often needs a slightly quirky yet inoffensive quality in order to be effective; just as the pop song is crafted with technique as well as inspiration, so too is library music. And the same things apply here as elsewhere: you need to make contact and persevere in order to have any chance of success.

To find TV or film work without prior experience is difficult. In addition to the above, you need to have a pretty good technical knowledge of music, production and recording to have a chance. Many people start off by writing library music as a stepping stone to these more lucrative areas, and I'd recommend this route unless you're really confident in your abilities. If you're successful in finding a publisher who is prepared to place some of your library music on TV, this can be very much to your advantage when trying to find a way in.

Summary

So, to sum up, there are no straightforward ways to get on in the business. Even if you're exceptionally talented, you'll almost certainly need to be flexible regarding the kind of work you're prepared to do, and most successful professionals have a number of different revenue streams. However, it can take only one phone call – often completely unexpected – for something to change. A lot of the best work I've had has occurred this way, sometimes through people I'd met only once or twice, so if you're determined to follow the life of a professional musician, remember that. And, above all, don't stop trying!

13 SAMPLING AND THE STUDIO

'What did we start? I like to think that we did do different things with sampling.'
– *Anne Dudley on her time in the Art Of Noise*

'In the studio I don't think you can ever know enough about what you're doing.' – *Al Stone, producer, Jamiroquai*

Keyboard playing and technology go hand in hand. From the very first synthesisers through to today's sophisticated electronic music setups, the controlling instrument of choice has always been the keyboard. As a keyboard player yourself, this gives you access to a massively powerful and fascinating musical world, which was touched on in *Part 1*. (Again, if you haven't already read this, I strongly urge you to find a copy.)

As you develop your musical skills further, the twin aspects of playing and producing sounds become ever more closely related. Technology gets really interesting when it fires up your creative imagination and makes you think of new ways of doing something, and over the next few pages we'll take a look at how technology can help you in a number of different ways.

Understanding how to hook up your instrument to your computer is one thing, but using and making sense of all the possibilities you then have access to can appear be a bit of a nightmare at first. But there's no need to be a technophile to enjoy using the amazing equipment available today; it's surprising how effectively you can write and record music, or develop new sounds, with fairly modest gear. This is something we now take for granted, but we owe the basis of much of today's technology to an earlier era, and this is especially true in a particularly important area of technological development that has transformed music over the last 20 years or so: sampling.

Sampling Technology

It's fair to say that sampling has permanently changed the face of music. However, the term *sampling* is used so widely these days that many people are unsure of what it actually means. Sampling simply allows you to record something digitally and then play it back by means of triggering sounds from a keyboard or (more typically these days) via a sequencing program. Whether you have some or no knowledge of the subject, it's very useful to understand how early sampling was achieved and how it has evolved into today's vital tool.

Sampling Development

It's comes as no great surprise that advances in sampling have gone hand in hand with the development of digital technology. For instance, the first moderately useful hardware samplers were developed in the early 1980s, when digital systems and circuits began to become more available.

Two of the most popular early samplers were the Fairlight and the Emulator. The Emulator, in particular, looked just like a regular keyboard, despite its wealth of sound-producing capabilities. What you could do with it, though, was revolutionary at the time: you could plug an instrument, microphone or indeed any sound source into it with just a regular jack lead, then press the Record button on the Emulator and it would digitally record whatever you played into it. You could then play back the sound using the Emulator's keyboard. And, of course, you could record absolutely anything you liked – a piano, a vocal line, a drum groove, someone speaking or a dog barking – and if you listen to a few '80s synth bands you'll hear that they *did* sample just about everything.

You could also play back the samples on the Emulator's keyboard at varying pitches. However, the higher up the keys you played, the faster the sound, which gave a Mickey Mouse effect similar to that involved with speeding up a tape. Conversely, the lower down the keyboard (below the pitch of the original sample) you played, the slower the sample would be. This effect was often quite a large problem, depending on the type of sound that had been sampled, but the overall result was the same: the tone and character would be changed if you went more than a few notes above or below the original sample. The answer was to make several samples of the sound – for instance, when sampling a grand piano, you would take a sample every fourth or fifth note to give a realistic sound when playing back the sound on the sampler. This technique is still used today, and is a process known as *multisampling*.

So far, so good. But while the Fairlight and the Emulator were both pioneers of a new technology, they were, in their original forms, impractical and of rather limited abilities. Firstly, they were both prohibitively expensive (particularly the Fairlight) and handicapped by having only a small amount of memory. This meant that only a short sample time was available, and as all of both machines' onboard data was lost when they were switched off, samples had to be saved onto removable disks (which had nothing like the capacity of today's storage media). So they were initially niche machines usually bought by wealthy artists or expensive studios, who could offset the time (and cost) needed to load and save samples.

The Digital Age

Technology develops at a frightening rate, however, and on the horizon were digital samplers for the masses, machines that could be bought at reasonable cost and gave ordinary musicians a chance to try out this revolutionary new technology. While there were several initial attempts, the first really groundbreaking sampler was the Akai S900, developed in the mid-'80s. Designed as a keyboardless module equipped with a MIDI interface and a form of multitimbral operation, it helped to spawn a new generation of musicians who made history by sampling and producing records in their bedrooms. At the time, there was no other remotely effective competitor, which meant that the Akai brand name became synonymous with samplers in general. The company continues to develop its sampling instruments today.

However, while it might have opened new musical doors, the S900 was still a relatively limited device. It could sample only in mono, and the total amount of sampling time that the onboard memory could support was only something like 20 seconds at a reasonable bandwidth (don't worry, this is explained later). While it would allow you to perform basic editing tasks such as looping (where part of a sample is played and then replayed and replayed, *ad infinitum*, in order to save memory) and making up multitimbral patches of samples, it wasn't long before more highly developed versions eclipsed it.

Nevertheless, in many core respects, the modern samplers available today are merely more powerful, more highly developed versions of the S900. They all operate on the same principle in that, once you've sampled a sound, you can then edit it on the sampler by deciding which bits of the sample you want to keep and then storing them, either on a floppy disk, on an internal hard drive (similar to the one on a home computer) or on some other format, such as a Zip drive.

Generally, the kinds of tasks for which people use hardware samplers like these are twofold. One is to sample a selection of notes from another instrument and use those to create a *patch* (or sound) that can be played just like a sound on a regular keyboard. The other is to sample sections of music – a drum groove, for instance – and use this to make up the basis of a rhythm track by triggering it at the start of each bar. Traditionally, this is one of the most widely used methods for making up dance tracks.

But sampling, and indeed recording in general, has moved on a lot in recent years. While hardware samplers still have their uses, there is now a much neater way of recording digitally, one that uses a household object we've encountered already: the home computer.

Recording MIDI And Audio With A Multitrack Sequencer

In *100 Tips For Keyboards Part 1*, I looked at how it's possible to hook any MIDI-equipped keyboard up to your computer, given the right hardware. The type of software you need to use here is called a *multitrack sequencer*, of which there are many different brands and types, the most popular being Cubase VST and SX (made by Steinberg) and Logic (made by Emagic). While there are operating differences between the two, they both do the same thing: allow you to record and play back MIDI information. If you have a multitimbral MIDI keyboard or module, you can use it to record several separate tracks with different sounds and then play them all back together, making up a very full-sounding track. However, in addition to recording MIDI information, Cubase, Logic and most modern multitrack sequencers can also record audio data. The audio tracks can then be viewed on the main Arrange page of the program, along with the MIDI tracks, which makes it very easy for you to see instantly what's going on, as all the tracks scroll across the screen horizontally while you're playing.

There are several advantages in recording certain types of audio using your computer rather than a hardware sampler. Firstly, audio uses up a lot of memory, and while a modern hardware sampler is infinitely more powerful than the old S900, it can't hold a candle to a desktop computer's performance. Secondly, any audio you record on your computer is stored instantly on its internal hard drive, making it a much quicker and more straightforward process.

Perhaps most relevantly, however, the array of processing and editing functions that a desktop computer and sequencing program allow you to perform on an audio file provides you with a much greater degree of flexibility than you could possibly get from a hardware sampler. You can speed the file up, slow it down, copy and paste it, apply processing such as equalisation to it – the list is endless.

So here we'll have a look at how to get audio onto your computer, and how to use it in conjunction with the MIDI tracks you can record using your keyboard.

As with MIDI, a computer needs an interface in order to allow it to be connected to audio equipment. This is usually a fairly painless procedure, as most computers are sold with an adequate soundcard. While you can spend a lot of money to get a soundcard with a superior audio specification, a cheap Soundblaster or the like will do perfectly well to get you started.

At the back of the card will be a selection of audio sockets (often mini-jacks, in the case of cheaper soundcards). One of these sockets will be designed to accept audio in, while another will send audio out. Both will be stereo sockets, so you might need to acquire specific cables to connect up your audio source to the card. You can then run your soundcard's outputs through your hi-fi or (better) a mixing desk to hear the audio.

Sampling Rates And Disk Space
Once you've connected everything up, take a look at the Preferences or Setup menu in your sequencer program. There will probably be an option there to choose which sample rate you wish to use.

Like anything else, audio always requires space in which to be stored, whether this is on a cassette tape or on a computer's hard drive. When audio is recorded digitally, the amount of memory or hard disk space it uses up is determined by a few key factors, such as whether the audio is recorded in stereo or mono; whether it's recorded at 16-, 24- or 32-bit resolution; and the sampling rate (measured in kHz), or the number of times the signal is measured per second. All these combine to determine the quality of the recording.

CDs use a sampling rate of 44.1kHz, and while I wouldn't recommend using a rate lower than this, it's still a perfectly acceptable number. Likewise, a lower resolution than 16-bit can result in a noticeable drop-off in recording quality. Higher sampling rates, such as 96kHz and 192kHz, are appearing increasingly often on better-specified soundcards, but you should be aware that not only do these higher rates gobble up more space on your hard drive, but you might also be hard pressed to hear the difference.

Starting A Recording
Before recording audio onto your sequencer, first of all you should name the track, after which you can select whether it's to be recorded in stereo or mono. Most programs also have a Mixer page where it's easy to tell whether or not an audio signal is being received by your soundcard. If it is, you should be ready to record a few bars. Put your sequencing program into Record mode and off you go.

When you stop playing and press the Stop button on the sequencer's graphic interface, the audio track will probably appear on the Wave Edit page as a squiggly wave-like graphic. This image actually describes the data quite accurately, because part of the process of recording audio onto your computer requires it to be converted into a digital waveform. This audio file is now stored on your hard drive, and you can do what you want with it – save it along with the main song, delete it, re-record it or edit it. The number of audio tracks that your sequencer can handle will depend upon several factors, including the quality of your hardware, but most can manage up to 16 mono tracks quite comfortably.

While there are many more avenues to explore in the field of audio recording, you should by now have a mini-recording studio at your disposal.

Dealing With Files
Audio files are usually saved as either of two specific types. If you use a PC, they will be saved as WAV files, while on a Mac they will be stored as AIFF files. Most Macs can read WAV files and convert them into AIFFs, just as PCs can convert AIFFs into WAVs. In either case, though, at the end of the day they're computer files, which means that you have a vast range of possibilities. We'll look at some of these in a moment.

Before we do, though, let's try to get this whole process of dealing with computer recording – both MIDI and digital audio – into perspective. Whenever you deal with digital data, it's just that: data. You already know that MIDI is just a form of information, that it's not sound itself; essentially, it's just a string of numbers telling a bit of gear that it has to perform a task, which could be anything from playing a note to changing a sound. When audio gets recorded onto your computer's hard drive, it's converted from (usually) an analogue signal into a digital waveform – which, again, is merely data. To be heard as music, it has to be played back using a specially designed program (such as a multitrack sequencer) and fed out of the soundcard to an amplifier and speakers.

As you probably know from using standard word-processing programs on your computer, you can do an awful lot with data – cut out bits of it, copy it, paste it or put it into other programs that read the same type of file format. While an audio file might be a hell of a lot bigger than a text file, it's really only a different type of computer file. When you fully take this concept on board, it makes it much easier to understand how it's possible to do so much with digital audio.

Let's go back to the audio recording you did a little while ago. After you stopped the sequencer, the track should have appeared on the main Arrange page as a segment, just like a MIDI track. Within this Arrange page you can move the audio track around to your heart's content, dragging and dropping it into any part of the song, or by copying and pasting it to a different location. It's not hard to realise that this kind of editing functionality can make constructing a song a very simple matter and can open up a wide range of possibilities.

Processing Audio Files And Plugins

Now we're really starting to get into the area where the power of your computer starts to become a major factor. The term *audio processing* refers to the alteration, or treatment, of an audio track, and over the years audio processing has become an integral part of recording. The most basic, and common, types of processing are some that you might already have encountered – effects such as reverberation, echo/delay, equalisation, chorus and so on. Many of today's keyboards come with onboard effects like these which you can apply to the instrument's sounds, whereas just a few years ago the only effects available were boxes of outboard gear, separate units that usually stood in an impressive-looking rack case, each of which had to be connected up to a mixing desk (or other means of feeding a signal in and out, such as an effects loop on an instrument amplifier). As well as consuming a lot of physical space, the useability of separate units like these was restricted if you didn't have a large enough mixing desk to run them all at the same time.

In addition to the aforementioned basic effects, there are countless other forms of processing available, and we'll be looking at these at a little later on. What you need to know now is that the power of a modern computer allows you to do away with these separate effects boxes, if you wish. You can now process all of your audio within your computer by applying digital effects to the audio tracks in the sequencer program. While this hasn't exactly made outboard gear redundant, most of it now caters for the higher ends of the market, because being able to process audio within a computer is easy, convenient, and it works pretty well.

You'll find that some effects will be contained within the sequencer package, while you can also import other effects, known as *plugins*, which will run alongside your sequencer program. The procedure for finding an effects (or *FX* for short) section in a sequencer package will vary from program to program, but there will usually be an FX button on the screen near where you would type in the name of the audio track on the Arrange page. Clicking on this will normally launch a separate window providing various options concerning which effects you want turned on or off and the amount of level you want to send to each one. (You can normally select a range of effects from one of the main menus that drop down from the top of the

page. Try 'Panels' or 'Options'. If you get lost, refer to the user manual for guidance.)

The principle here is to get you started, so I won't go into too much detail about using the various forms of FX. For now, just experiment and see how many different types of sound you can produce. There's one thing you'll notice fairly quickly, though: the drain that using onboard FX has on your computer's processor. The fact is that audio processing requires a lot of memory and computing power; the more audio tracks you use, and the more FX you use, the quicker you'll notice a slow-down in general computer operation to the point where, in extreme circumstances, the computer will stop playing the sequencer entirely. Most modern computers can take on a very high workload before they do this, but while using FX can be fun and can transform the sound of even quite humble recordings, it's worth remembering not to overdo it.

We're going to return to this area and look more closely at making music once we've had a quick look at integrating all this equipment so that it works for you. For now, though, here's a brief look around the rest of the studio.

A Quick Tour Of The Studio

While the prospect of being able to do so much within your computer can be exciting, it can sometimes be restricting to work entirely in the virtual domain, so I'd always recommend using a mixture of hardware and software, for reasons I'll come to shortly.

It's impossible to get away from the fact that one piece of hardware at the heart of a good setup – in the studio or live – is the mixing desk. *100 Tips For Keyboards Part 1* looked closely at using a desk to give you a good live sound using a small six- or eight-channel version with two auxiliary sends. As we're exploring the area of recording again here, though, we're going to look at slightly different types of desks, which, although larger, still operate on much the same principle.

You can find yourself needing some sort of desk at quite an early stage in your recording. While it's possible to use a separate keyboard combo amp, or to run the signal straight into your hi-fi, as soon as you need to connect up more than one or two pieces of equipment and hear them at the same time, you're sunk. And this serves as a good illustration of the role of a mixing desk: it's a meeting place, a junction, through which many pieces of equipment can be heard at the same time. When you get deeper into audio recording, though, you'll soon find out that you need rather more than this.

If you want to record two tracks of audio onto your computer using a basic desk, it's quite simple. You take an output from either the main stereo outs or the auxiliaries and plug the cables into your soundcard. However, you have the capability on your sequencer program to record many more than two audio tracks at a time, and you might also want to record one instrument on one track, another on a second, mix two or more channels onto a third – an infinite amount of possibilities exist. In short, you need to be able to send different sounds to your computer out of separate outputs.

This requirement for a separate output section determined the make-up of mixing desks long before computers were used to make music. The common configuration of an input section (like that on a small live desk) and a separate output section (known as a *subgroup*) became a popular choice for sending out signals to multitrack tape recorders, and is still the basis for the construction of recording desks today. Of course, desks come in all shapes and sizes, right up to the massive models you see in the top studios. But, whatever the size, a recording desk will work on the same principle: in addition to its input channels, in order to be truly flexible, it must also have a subgroup section with separate outputs.

Analogue And Digital Desks
Analogue Desks
The small live desk described above is classed as an *analogue* desk, which means – from a user's point of view – that each function has its own dedicated control, be it a knob, slider or button, which makes this type of desk relatively easy to understand and get to grips with.

Typical home or small studio recording desks are split up into three sections – input, subgroup and master output – with, for instance 16 input channels, eight separate subgroup output sockets and a stereo master output section. The input sections on most models are in most respects identical to those on many small live desks (described in more detail in *Part 1*), apart from one main feature: each input channel will have a row of numbered buttons which, when depressed, send the signal in that numbered channel along the desk to the equivalent output socket. You would then need to run a lead from that output socket to your computer soundcard. For example, depressing button 1 would send the signal to the first separate output, button 2 would send the signal to the second, and so on. Of course, you can send the same signal to all eight separate outs if you want, or a combination of signals from any of the 16 input channels, in a process known as *routing*, or *assigning*.

It's a very flexible system, ideal for multitrack recording.

Digital Desks
The digital desk is a slightly different animal. For a start, it's a bit smaller than its analogue cousin, with very few

knobs on the front panel; instead, the various controls of the desk are accessed via a series of onscreen menus. This makes simple things like adjusting equalisation and panning a little less intuitive than on an analogue console, though not as hard to get used to as you might expect.

Where the digital desk *does* score is in terms of features. The analogue desk doesn't usually contain any significant means of processing a signal, requiring you to connect up separate outboard gear, whereas the digital desk usually has a substantial array of onboard effects that can be applied to any input channel. Not just the basic reverb, delay and chorus, either – often more serious studio tools, such as compression and noise gates, are thrown in for good measure.

The other trump card that a digital desk offers is its ability to save and recall mixes. Digital desks allow you to save complete *snapshots* that memorise positions of faders, EQ, effects – virtually everything. So, if you want to move between songs that have completely different settings, you can save a mix and move on to the next one knowing that you can recall your saved mix at any time.

When it comes to a separate subgroup section, a digital desk often has several options. Instead of having a series of output sockets, digital desks have slots on their rear panels which allow you to insert cards containing various types of interface. You can opt for a traditional series of analogue input and output sockets, or you can use a digital card that accepts digital XLR, optical or coaxial cables. Like most other features on a digital desk, assignment is done via a series of menus, which personally I don't mind, although many prefer the more visible, hands-on approach you get with an analogue desk.

Hooking A Desk Up To A Soundcard
So we now have a means of getting a number of separate signals out of a mixing desk, ready to be recorded. How far you can now go depends on the specification of your soundcard. A cheap Soundblaster-type card, as described earlier, will get you started with basic audio recording, but it will probably have only one stereo input, so if you want to take in the separate outs from a mixer, you'll need to purchase a (slightly) more expensive card that will accept multiple inputs. Currently, these cards can be found from around £100 ($180) upwards, and typically they will accept series of either analogue inputs (the leads coming from your analogue mixer's subgroup section) or digital cables.

Digital recording interfaces come in many different formats, two of the most popular consumer varieties being A-DAT (which uses two optical cables, one in and one out) and TDIF (which uses two coaxial cables). With these digital interfaces, you just plug two cables into the input and output sockets on the digital card at the back of your mixer, then plug the other ends into their respective sockets on your soundcard. Each cable can then carry up to eight tracks' worth of recording data.

- **CAUTIONARY NOTE!** Either your soundcard or your mixing desk (but not both) must be set to send out a Word Clock signal, which can be carried through the cables already connecting the two devices. Failure to do this properly will result in the signal being corrupted with glitches and pops, which can spoil your recording.

So, as you can see, while you'll need a digital mixer (and a soundcard with a digital interface) to connect up to your computer digitally, you can still hook up quite happily with an analogue desk.

Opinions vary about the relative merits of analogue versus digital recording. Personally, I think there are far too many factors involved to get into that debate here. However, the ability to recall mixes and the onboard effects present on digital desks can make them a more suitable choice for use with a computer music system. That said, though, you should never underestimate the ability of older equipment to do a good job.

Effects And Processing – A Quick Breakdown

These days, digital processors and effects can be found on board mixing desks, on your keyboard, as computer plugins and as outboard gear, and what follows is a brief list of some of the most common effects:

- **Reverberation (Reverb)** – This is perhaps the most widely used effect in both live and recording situations. Natural reverberation occurs when sound carries around large internal spaces, like cathedrals, bouncing off the hard reflective surfaces so often the reflections blur together. (I could have said 'echoes' rather than 'carries', but echo refers to another specific effect, which shouldn't be confused with reverb.)

  The reverberation in a cathedral is an extreme example, as it lasts for several seconds, but a digital reverb program or unit will contain patches that can replicate anything from long reverb times like this to very short, almost imperceptible ones. The most common use of reverb is to add a little depth to a sound, sometimes without it being very apparent. Indeed, many keyboard sounds benefit from a moderate amount of reverb – but be careful not to overdo it when applying it to regular sounds.

As well as varying the reverb time, it's also possible to alter the mix of the reverberated and original, 'dry' signal in order to increase or decrease the amount of reverb heard.

- **Echo** – Also known as *delay*, this effect often gets mixed up with the wrong terminology. The effect of echo, or delay, being applied to a sound is most easily understood by imagining yourself in a situation where the sound bounces from one surface to another, such as a cave or a valley; if you called out, the sound of your voice would be repeated several times, in a distinct number of echoes, before dying away.

  While many years ago studios used to use complex analogue echo units, modern echo-type effects are created by digital delay programs. A digital delay works, by, in effect, sampling the incoming sound and repeating it. Delay times can be selected from long to very short, with longer settings giving the effect of the sound being produced in a cave or valley and shorter settings producing slapback effects. A feedback control determines the number of times the delay repeats.

  Digital delays also have a feature known as a *modulator*, which can be used to create several other effects, such as chorus.

- **Chorus** – This is an effect designed to fatten up a sound by modulating it – ie by making the pitch waver slightly above and below the note. As the original dry sound is overlaid with this chorused effect, it can give the impression of more than one instrument playing, because of the constant but very subtle variation in pitch. You can vary the speed and depth of the chorus effect to give a greater or lesser effect as you desire. Chorusing can work very well on synth-string parts – particularly higher up the keyboard, where some string sounds can start to get a little weedy – and a slow, wide chorus can give extra width and depth to sustained sounds such as organ and brass patches.

- **Phasing** – Phasing effects can also be created by using the modulation feature in a delay program. The term *phasing* refers to the sound that results when two identical sounds are played simultaneously, placed 'on top' of each other. In the old days, two tape machines were run in synchronisation to achieve this, but today it's a simple matter to use a delay program to produce the same effect. Using a very short delay setting, you can mix the processed and the original dry sound to create a very distinctive sound. Slow rates of modulation particularly suit sounds such as string pads and ambient effects.

Compression

Compression is one of the less glamorous-sounding processes, but it's nevertheless a tool that's worth its weight in gold. Like many other pieces of electronic music gear, at one time compressors were all separate, stand-alone pieces of hardware that sat in racks. These days, compressor plugins are amongst the most widely used and popular forms of processing. To understand why, and what one can do for you, you first need to know some of its typical uses.

The dynamic range of most musical instruments and voices can be extreme, and in a recording environment (and, sometimes, live) levels that are either too high or too low can potentially ruin the sound. Most of you, I'm sure, will have heard an overloaded signal when recording a tape at too high a level, or the lack of presence when the recording level has been too low.

A compressor's job, very generally, is to compensate for this by reducing the level of a sound when it has reached a certain point. This can both prevent distortion and also help to deal with a difficult, peaky sound without the overall level being too low. In short, it squashes the sound into a smaller, more manageable dynamic range.

A compressor can be applied to a single channel or to an overall mix. Either way, basic controls do the same job:

- **Threshold** – Sets the point at which a compressor starts to reduce the level of a sound.

- **Ratio** – When a sound has exceeded the threshold and compression is kicking in, the larger the ratio, the more compression will be applied. Ratios can be selected from 1:1 (no compression) to infinity:1 (at which point no signal whatsoever will be allowed past the threshold point). When a compressor is used at this latter setting, it is performing the task of a limiter.

- **Hard/Soft Knee** – When a sound reaches the threshold, hard-knee compression is applied to all of the signal straight away, whereas soft-knee compression is introduced gradually, before the threshold is reached, and is often a more musical, less obviously compressed sound.

- **Attack** – Determines how quickly the compressor reacts when a sound has exceeded the threshold.

- **Release** – A user-defined release time can be applied to determine how quickly the compressor's level returns to normal when the sound has fallen below the threshold.

Compression can actually be a surprisingly creative tool; setting a slow attack time, for instance, can allow part of a percussive sound – such as a clav – to pass through uncompressed, accentuating its sharpness. While it's primarily a studio-based animal, compression can also be applied effectively to individual channels or the master output of a mixing desk when playing live.

Stand-Alone Hard-Disk Recorders

While I've concentrated here on recording audio using your computer, if you're looking for a similarly portable backup facility, a stand-alone hard-disk recorder might be worth considering. Most are standard studio-rack width (19") and are straightforward audio-recording devices, using a hard drive to store recordings. They can be connected via a range of different analogue or digital interfaces, and most can export the audio data on their hard drives as WAV files, which you can then import into a sequencer program. Some models can also can be hooked up to display monitors, allowing you to edit the audio on the recorder this way.

I'll be honest, though – I don't use my stand-alone recorder very much. However, it *is* useful to have the extra recording facility, which can help take the load off a computer system. Also, its portability means that you can take it out of your studio and record a live gig, for instance, which might not be something you'd readily contemplate with a computer.

Hard-disk recorders range from small units (which can typically record eight separate audio tracks) up to 24-track versions (which are often not that much more expensive than their smaller counterparts). It's possible to remove their hard drives, if you want to keep a whole disk's worth of recording, and insert a fresh one – not unlike replacing tape on a big multitrack recorder.

14 SOFT SYNTHS AND SAMPLING

'A rock band used to be four guys and a drummer. Now it's five guys sitting around reading manuals!' – *Bill Bruford*

'I think people, especially these days, get four bars, build that up and find another four bars to go with it –
then one's your verse and one's your chorus – and I don't find that particularly inspiring.
I like things to grow, in the same way as a conversation.' – *Neil Davidge, producer, Massive Attack*

In *100 Tips For Keyboards Part 1*, I covered some of the basic means of getting a MIDI signal into and out of your computer by using either a cable attached to your soundcard's joystick port or a more dedicated unit such as a USB interface. Once this has been done, it's then possible to record MIDI signals onto a sequencer program and output them via MIDI to whichever sound source you happen to be using.

However, there are a number of other sound-generating options that can be used in conjunction with your computer. One of these involves using software synths, or *soft synths*.

Soft Synths

A digital synthesiser, in its hardware form, uses digital waveforms to recreate a wide range of sounds. In many ways, it makes sense to put this digital information onto a software disk and run it from your computer, thus giving you the 'guts' of the physical keyboard synth (ie the mathematical data used to create various sounds) without having to clutter up your studio with large pieces of equipment.

While some soft synths come as complete stand-alone programs, the ones described here can be controlled from within the same sequencing program you use for normal MIDI and audio recording. In this instance, they will typically appear as options on your MIDI Track Output menu. You can then send a MIDI signal into the computer by playing a keyboard to trigger the soft synth. The synth will also have its own Edit panel, allowing you to make up and tailor your own sounds, thus bringing you ever closer to integrating your studio within your computer. It's also a fact that soft synths are significantly cheaper than their hardware counterparts, although in practice there's a wide variation of success with which various soft-synth packages work.

One problem is the sounds they produce. In theory, it should be possible to recreate the sound of any synthesiser ever produced, and yet some soft synths are distinctly better in this field than others. Soft-synth designers often favour trying to replicate the sound of some of the really old analogue synths from the '60s and '70s, which is an appealing idea because, as very few good examples of these instruments still exist – and they were all designed long before the days of MIDI – a soft synth equipped with these kinds of patches provides a great opportunity to use classic sounds in a modern environment.

The thing about older synthesisers, though, is that their older circuitry and occasionally stroppy behaviour were what gave them character and a unique type of sound, and these idiosyncrasies are captured better by some soft synths than others. The huge range of different soft-synth products out there can give you a massive library of sounds, though, and there are many really good-sounding products currently available.

The other major issue at stake is latency, which we'll come to in a moment.

Soft Samplers

Recording audio into your sequencer program is one way of integrating MIDI and audio within your computer, while another is to use a software sampler. There are many occasions, too, when a sampler fits your requirements far better than sequencing sections of audio.

As you might expect, a software sampler works on the same basic principle as a soft synth, using the processing power – and, in this case, the hard-disk capacity – of a desktop computer to give a very powerful and flexible alternative to a hardware sampler. It's integrated in much the same way into a typical sequencing program, such as Cubase or Logic. While a soft sampler will also have a separate menu for sampling, it should appear as a playback option in the same Track Output menu as a soft synth.

However, the way in which a soft sampler works is a little different to the hardware versions looked at earlier. On a hardware sampler, when you start recording, the sample is saved into the machine's internal RAM (Random Access Memory), which can be accessed very quickly so that, when you play a note, the sample associated with the key can be heard virtually immediately. The downside of this setup is the relatively small amount of RAM afforded by most hardware samplers, limiting the total sampling time available.

When a soft sampler records a section of audio, the data is stored straight onto the computer's hard drive, just as it is with audio sequencing. As the size of even the smallest computer hard drive is many, many times greater than the internal RAM of a hardware sampler, it's possible to record extremely long samples – in theory, right up to the capacity of your hard drive. When you want to play back these samples, they're read back from the hard drive in a process known as *streaming*. However, the computer's hard drive won't be able to respond quickly enough when a note is played (there's a short but noticeable delay before the sample can be accessed), so a small amount of the sample is loaded into the computer's RAM to compensate for this.

This gives you the best of both worlds: instant playback response and the huge storage space of your computer's hard drive. It sounds like a great way to approach sampling, and in many ways it is, although again you have to bear in mind the potential drain on your computer system.

Latency

Latency refers to the delay that's incurred between playing a note on a keyboard and hearing the required sound generated by a soft synth or sampler through a speaker or headphones. In severe cases, this latency can be serious enough to make playing very difficult.

Latency is largely a product of the buffer on your computer's soundcard. A large buffer size can help the card handle demanding situations, often when the computer is heavily loaded with various tasks. To get the lowest possible latency, however, you need to reduce the size of the soundcard buffer to as low as you can get away with. This will vary from computer to computer, and can only be done by trial and error, although, given the computing power of most modern systems, you should be able to achieve a latency of under 11 milliseconds, which will make any delay virtually unnoticeable.

However, you should be aware that, by lowering the computer's buffer size to achieve very low latency, you'll also be making computer less able to deal with occasional hiccups whenever its processor is heavily loaded. This can cause glitches and imperfections in a signal and a degradation of audio recording quality. As with most things, there is a compromise involved, I'm afraid, and here it is.

Saving Your Work

You can tell that your particular system is approaching the edge of its capabilities when it gets less and less responsive. It may even stop altogether. However, you can't always tell when it is going to crash. The more applications you have running at once, and the more your system struggles as a consequence, the more prone you are to this calamity.

If you're using soft synths and samplers, you have the added pain that they will all go down as well, so whatever you do, get into the habit of saving your files regularly.

Using Sampling CDs And CD-ROMs

One of the big advantages of having a good computer-based music system is that you can use thousands of commercially available sample-library discs containing samples that you can load into your audio sequencer or sampler, whether it's a hardware or software model.

These discs tend to fall into either of two categories: the sort that feature drum loops, vocal licks, ambient noises and other generally useful samples, and dedicated multi-disc libraries of orchestral instruments that have been painstakingly recorded. These latter library discs can be frighteningly expensive, and are specifically designed to be used with the sort of streaming soft sampler described earlier. The former, general library CDs tend to be reasonably cheap, however, and can be a great way of getting hold of sounds to put a track together. Most contain WAV files that can be imported straight into a track on your sequencer, so they're very easy to use out of the box.

15 BASIC PHILOSOPHY OF USING GEAR

'People shouldn't really get too hung up on any particular item. It really is to do with the way you
see sound and the way you position sound – the dynamics. It's a real light-and-shade thing.
It's the silences, the spaces. That's where the real melodies are.' – *William Orbit*

'Well, the things that I've held onto have certain features that I don't think I could recreate on anything else.
I've also grown fond of them, and at the same time they have virtually no resale value,
so there'd really be no point in getting rid of them!' – *Anne Dudley on vintage electronic gear*

When you're using any kind of recording gear, the kind of equipment you end up using is largely a function of what you want to do – and, of course, the size of your budget. It seems inescapable that computers are fast becoming the centre for most people's musical needs, and, as we've seen, using sequencers, soft synths, soft samplers and plugins means that you can now do more within your computer than ever before.

However, while everyone finds their own way of working, my advice would be to avoid putting all of your eggs in one basket. Sometimes we expect too much from a computer – whether this is through running too many applications or using software that doesn't quite manage to do what you want it to – so my advice is to be aware of what you can get out of all of your equipment – including older, semi-obsolete gear – before buying the latest soft synth or processing plugin. Older equipment isn't generally worth much anyway, so unless you really need the space, hang onto it because it might come in useful one day.

What counts is your approach to sound and, more specifically, the degree of control you can have over each device. At the end of the day, the only connection you have with all of the audio programs and sounds on your computer is through your soundcard, which might have only a limited amount of outputs. It's this fundamental factor that can make a big difference to the sound of your recordings.

This is why you're best off with a physical, hardware mixing desk at the centre of your setup. Sure, sequencer programs such as Cubase and Logic have onboard facilities allowing you to adjust the levels of each MIDI or audio track and make adjustments, but there are drawbacks here. Firstly, unless you can permanently bring up the mixer in a separate window (which is sometimes possible), you have to go into a menu and select it. Secondly, these selections have to be made onscreen, so you have to use your mouse or keyboard to make adjustments, which isn't a particularly hands-on way of doing things. Thirdly, on an onboard mixer, while you can apply EQ and effects to each audio track, it'll start to use up your system resources. And finally, of course, you might also be sending out MIDI information to several keyboards or sound modules, which all need to go through some kind of mixing system in order to be heard.

With this being the case, I recommend that you share out the duties a little. Using a hardware mixer (either analogue or digital) has several advantages. While the size of the model is determined by your own requirements, basically a 16-input-channel desk with an eight-channel subgroup section should give you quite a bit of room to expand. Inputs have a habit of being used up surprisingly quickly; many synths and keyboards, for example, have separate outputs in addition to their stereo ones, all of which need to go into separate input channels on your desk.

Once you've got the signals running into your desk, you can then apply EQ, panning or effects using the auxiliary sends. It's this control of separate outputs that can be a major factor in improving your sound.

You can also return the outputs from your soundcard back through the input channels on the hardware desk. If you have multiple outputs, this can eat up your input channels, making you appreciate the benefit of having a reasonably sized desk very quickly! The advantage with this way of working, though, is that you then have other options for mixing the audio tracks from your computer. While these tracks can still be adjusted from the sequencer's onboard mixer, returning them through a hardware desk means that you have more hands-on control (if you desire it) and you don't need to rely on the computer to do everything; you can use the EQ and processing on your hardware desk instead, taking some of the burden away from your computer's CPU. If you can afford a digital desk, you can also memorise your mix settings, which can really add to your system's flexibility.

You should therefore consider the following when you're deciding on how to set up your system:

- If you agree that a hardware desk is a good idea, try to obtain a digital one. It's possible to find good, useable, second-hand examples for around £500 ($900) or more, and if you're lucky you can find one that has a recording interface as well for that money.

- The performance of a computer is so dependent on the hardware fitted to it that it's impossible to give a good minimum specification. However, if you can, try to get a system that has been specifically designed for music use. You then stand the best chance of getting a well-matched system with good soundcard performance.

- Don't throw away your old gear for the sake of it, unless you absolutely have to. You might need it some day.

- If your keyboard is limited in sounds and facilities, consider purchasing another keyboard or module before looking at soft synths. Having something physical to play and operate can make your setup more flexible, which helps when something breaks down...

- Learn to get the most out of your current gear in addition to looking at new avenues. Understanding techniques such as using separate outputs and learning how sounds work with each other can lead to your music having a new lease of life.

APPENDIX: WORDS OF WISDOM

- Buying equipment can be highly addictive, but try to buy only what you actually need. Don't create a need for it in the first place.

- Buy good cases for your equipment – believe me, you won't regret it.

- Look after your back. Sitting or standing while playing, mixing or driving takes its toll, as does carrying heavy equipment. If it's too heavy, get help when lugging gear around.

- There's no substitute for regular practice. Try to do some every day, even if for just a few minutes.

- Always make the toilet your last port of call before going onstage. To be stuck out there in agony is one of life's most unpleasant experiences!

- If you're a working musician, make sure your car is in good working order. It's as important as any other bit of equipment you'll ever have.

- Sometimes, learning and practising is a bit like being on a diet: you know that you could get down to it and progress if you really, really wanted to, so you'll make a start tomorrow, right? Wrong, of course. The way to keep your interest up here is to do something every day.

- Be receptive to forms of music that you don't like much on first hearing, or don't normally listen to. If you constantly listen to the same type of music, your playing can stagnate.

- If you're determined to forge a career in music, you'll need persistence in addition to talent.